Ridley Press

Becoming Eve

Requests for information should be addressed to:

susanshepherd1224@gmail.com

ISBN 978-1519549600

Editor: Nat Belz

Cover and interior design: Nat Belz

Cover photography: Shutterstock

Printed in the United States of America

For my Mom,
who taught me
to depend desperately
on the Word.

Becoming Eve

Recovering God's
Good Design
for Womanhood

by Susan Shepherd

"Ezer"

The following are occasions of the Hebrew word *ezer* from the Old Testament. The word *ezer* is #05828 in Strong's Concordance and it means "one who helps/helper." The **bold** instances are in reference to God.

Genesis 2:18 *Then the LORD God said, "It is not good that the man should be alone; I will make him a helper fit for him."*

Genesis 2:20 *The man gave names to all livestock and to the birds of the heavens and to every beast of the field. But for Adam there was not found a helper fit for him.*

Exodus 18:4 *The God of my Father was my* **help**, *and delivered me from the sword of Pharaoh.*

Deuteronomy 33:7 *And this he said of Judah: "Hear, O LORD, the voice of Judah, and bring him in to his people. With your hands contend for him, and be a* **help** *against his adversaries.*

Deuteronomy 33:26 *There is none like God, O Jeshurun, who rides through the heavens to your* **help**, *through the skies in his majesty.*

Deuteronomy 33:29 *Happy are you, O Israel! Who is like you, a people saved by the LORD, the shield of your* **help**, *and the sword of your triumph!*

Psalm 20:1, 2 *May the Lord answer you in the day of trouble! May the name of the God of Jacob protect you! May he send you* **help** *from the sanctuary and give you support from Zion!*

Psalm 33:20 *Our soul waits for the LORD; he is our* **help** *and our shield.*

Psalm 54:4 *Behold, God is my* **helper**; *the Lord is the upholder of my life.*

Psalm 70:5 *But I am poor and needy; hasten to me, O God! You are my* **help** *and my deliverer; O LORD, do not delay!*

Psalm 89:19 *Of old you spoke in a vision to your godly one, and said: "I have granted* **help** *to one who is mighty; I have exalted one chosen from the people.*

Psalm 115:9-11 *Israel, trust in the LORD! He is their* **help** *and their shield. O house of Aaron, trust in the LORD! He is their* **help** *and their shield. You who fear the LORD, trust in the LORD! He is their* **help** *and their shield.*

Psalm 121:2 *I lift up my eyes to the hills? Where does my* **help** *come from? My* **help** *comes from the LORD.*

Psalm 124:8 *Our* **help** *is in the name of the LORD, who made heaven and earth.*

Psalm 146:5 *Blessed is he whose* **help** *is the God of Jacob, whose hope is in the LORD his God.*

Isaiah 30:5 *Everyone comes to shame through a people that cannot profit them, that brings neither help nor profit, but shame and disgrace.*

Ezekiel 12:14 *And I will scatter toward every wind all who are around him, his helpers and all his troops, and I will unsheathe the sword after them.*

Daniel 11:34 *When they stumble, they shall receive a little* **help**.

Hosea 13:9 *He destroys you, O Israel, for you are against me, against your* **helper.**

Chapter One

MOUNTAINS AND MOLEHILLS

Chas, my steady, faithful, and funny husband of thirty years, is a great dad and a fully committed husband who is my biggest fan. He has contributed to my ministry in ways that I cannot even define. He has been deeply formative with both of our children, my own brothers, and many other young men who have worked with him over the years. This past year we watched both of our children walk down the aisle. What a privilege to have such a good marriage! I am forever grateful for the gift of our life together.

Yet our story is not without its disappointments. Almost twenty-five years ago, several days before Christmas, our little family gathered around the advent wreath to hear from God's Word and light the candle. My then two-year-old Hannah was enamored by the ritual but had no idea of its significance. She stood on a chair between her daddy and me while Chas read the little devotion for the night, and then read the Scripture. Following the instructions, he encouraged us to sing "Away in a Manger" together. Hannah loved to sing, so we launched into the first verse.

"Away in a manger, no crib for a bed. The little Lord Jesus, lay down his sweet head...."

I don't know about you, but sometimes, when I feel awkward, my instinctive reaction is to laugh. For some reason, our little family standing there singing "Away in a Manger" in the quiet of our living room made me feel awkward. And I laughed. Ugh.

My sweet husband responded, "Well, that's the last time I will do that." And it was. Chas never led devotions for our family again.

As I reflect on that evening, I don't believe that my reaction was one of rebellion or disrespect. It really was just a nervous response. But in that moment I robbed my husband of his rightful place as the leader of our home. My apparent disdain stole his confidence and the respect that he deserved. And that moment informed the next 25+ years of our marriage.

Molehill or Mountain?

You might be wondering, "What's the big deal? Seriously, Susan? This is a classic mountain/molehill thing. You need to get over it. One slip, almost 30 years ago, should not define your marriage." And maybe you would be right. Chas, by the way, has only a dim recollection of this event and was a bit surprised by how seriously it has hit me.

Honestly, I'm not sure that moment defined our marriage, but my response to that scene has characterized much of my life as a wife and mother, and that makes me incredibly sad. Over the years, I excluded Chas from the spiritual nurture of our children. It is, perhaps, a significant detail that during this time I served as the Director of Children's Ministry at our church. Who better to lead devotions for our kids than me? Who, indeed.

I'm not exactly sure how this happened. It's not as if I set out to take over, to "lead" our family in any way, to be self-sufficient. It just seemed to work. In contrast to Chas, I was raised in a Christian home. I had "biblical" training. I read the child-rearing and marriage books (apparently not the right books). I was the family expert. The marriage expert. The spiritual expert. And he was busy. So I just sort of took over. And it worked. After a fashion, and for a while.

You already know that our family is flourishing, so this story has a happy ending. By His marvelous grace, God has gradually and faithfully revealed the effect of my failure that December evening and in the intervening years. Our children are grown now, both beginning families of their own. It has largely been their journey that has informed my faith in this arena. Their honest questions as they navigate their own relationships, together with the convicting presence of the Holy Spirit, have peeled away layers of what I now see as my self-promoting and self-preserving womanhood. What I found, to my dismay, was a desperately wicked heart in need of transformation. I had an uninformed perspective of feminine godliness and, perhaps more importantly, a basic disconnect between my thinking faith and my practical life.

My ignorance was not due to lack of training. My mother reared six children in a home characterized by her own walk with God and her love for my dad. She was not Mother Teresa, and her marriage to my father was not perfect. But my mom loved Jesus and her life was a visible demonstration of her commitment to Christ, to the church and to her family. However, even in the shadow of my mother's godliness, I did not have much knowledge about what it means to be a godly woman. While I watched my mother closely over the years, and aspired to be like her in many ways, her godly womanhood somehow missed me completely.

Some of my earliest memories are of church and Sunday school. In my early adulthood I became a leader for a women's Bible study. During different seasons of my life, I studied passages about godly womanhood: Proverbs 31, Ephesians 5, 1 Peter 3, 1 Timothy 2 (not my favorite). If asked, I would have affirmed godly womanhood as a "good goal" for sanctification. I would have offered a list, or a profile, of what a godly woman should be. The profile would include (but not be limited to) the following:

Submissive

Respectful

Quiet

Gentle

Some lesser qualities might include serving, hospitable, not distracted by outward appearance, and not given to gossip. Even as I read that list now, I smile on the inside because I know that person is *so not me*. Who was I kidding?

What I did not know is that these texts, considered without the context of the whole counsel of Scripture and my relationship to Christ, led me to isolated applications that might fix my behavior rather than transform my heart and mind. Should I be submissive, respectful, quiet, and gentle? Clearly. But 1) I did not realize that my list fell woefully short of God's plan for *womanhood* and 2) I did not understand that my strategies to become that woman routinely failed after only a few days (or hours) because they were not connected to my *faith*.

My uninformed perspective of feminine godliness needed a good dose of biblical reality laced heavily with grace. God's design for gender identity is much bigger, much more significant, much richer and deeper than a list of things for me to do. His vision for what it means to be a *woman* who is His disciple and friend is not just about changing my behavior. It is about Jesus changing me.

Molehill or mountain? See what you think.

The Terrifying Sound of My Own Voice

I have read dozens of books on the subject of what it means to be a godly woman, and while I've learned a great deal, I've been surprised by the disregard of many Christian authors for their husbands and brothers – for the male species in general.

Just a cursory glance at Facebook® offers plenty of examples of women who are quick to mock and/or criticize their husbands. Status remarks like: "I sent 'Mike' to the store for whipping cream and he actually came home with Cool Whip®. This is why it is easier to do everything ourselves." Followed by these comments: "Actually, I think that's why they do it. So we will stop asking them to do things," and "The truth is that I doubt they know the difference. So why bother."

One episode of "Everybody Loves Raymond" reveals its title as a misnomer. Ray, whom "everybody loves," is typecast as an unthinking, unfeeling, disengaged, television-watching, sports-loving mama's boy. Debra, his wife, is smarter, kinder, more savvy, and productive. She corrects him, condescends to him, and dismisses him *in every episode.* If Debra's relationship with Ray is "love," it's no wonder this generation is slow to marry.

These examples are not meant to cast aspersions on the "world out there." This is too often my own posture. Debra's disdain for Ray too often mirrors my own – for my husband, my brothers, our pastors, for men in general.

I didn't even know the scorn existed in my heart and mind. I am not typically sarcastic and condescending. In public, I have always been sensitive about my portrayal of Chas, of our pastors or my brothers. God has gracefully shown me that what has been true in my own heart is perhaps more insidious because

I'm the only one that knows about it.

I did not know it was happening, but my ignorance is no excuse for my sin.

My Voice Has an Echo

This issue of disdain for men, of prideful independence, of haughty condescension, is not a singularly personal matter. The voice that emanates from my sinful heart has an echo that reverberates throughout our culture in ways that are far more worrisome than snide Facebook® commentary or sarcastic sitcom humor. In *Recovering Biblical Manhood & Womanhood*, Wayne Grudem describes the sociological impact that such gender malice between men and women leaves as its legacy on the next generation. If you think that my story is poignantly sad and obviously instructive for *me* – but such malice doesn't apply to or affect you – consider this (very) brief perspective of its impact on your world:

From 1973 through 2011, nearly 53 million legal abortions have occurred in the United States.[1] When we fail to live in the context of God's redemptive plan for gender (men and women!), we presume ownership of our bodies that is not ours. We boldly and unapologetically exercise our "independence" and autonomy from men and, ultimately, from God. We give ourselves permission to do whatever we want.

The United States Department of Labor reports that 51.5% of all workers in the high-paying management, professional, and related occupations are women. And that number is growing because women are now 33% more likely than men to receive college degrees.

Without undervaluing education and/or professional ad-

1 Latest year that CDC statistics are available according to www.abort73.com

vancement for women *and* men, it is significant that one result of such a trend is that 35% of mothers who work full-time are paying for childcare.[2] In a typical week during the spring of 2011, 12.5 million (61%) children under 5 years of age were in some type of regular child care arrangement. We are, as a nation, losing the value of family responsibility to raise our children.[3] And that is due in part to our refusal to live in the context of God's redemptive plan for gender.

In general, over the past twenty years, our country has:

- softened its position on crime, as the criminal has become the victim to be helped and not punished
- eliminated "competition" from children's sports so that everyone plays and every player is a winner,
- launched an effort to eliminate class distinctions, forcing economic equality and encouraging large-scale dependence on the government
- normalized a reversal of "traditional" male and female roles in the home.[4]

You may not immediately acknowledge the connection of these trends to our refusal to live in the context of God's design for men and women, but look carefully. Do you see the influence of women here and have we gone too far?[5] Can you trace the vehement demand for equality that women in our country have raised as our banner for the past twenty years resonating in these issues?

2 https://www.census.gov/prod/2013pubs/p70-135.pdf
3 I am very aware that many, if not most women who are working with their children in childcare are doing so out of necessity. I am not making a moral statement. My suggestion is that even this is, in some way, particularly related to our history of gender rebellion as a culture – it's a challenging connection to make, but it is definitely there.
4 *Biblical Foundations for Manhood and Womanhood*, p. 60-65
5 Here I am not suggesting that a woman's influence on these issues is inherently evil, but that the influence of women on these issues has, perhaps, been less than beneficial to our society in general.

Sisters, do not miss this. Whatever your personal position on the matters described above, these are the subtle consequences of our collective gender rebellion (male and female!). It is easy to spot the dramatic trends, like homosexuality. But the homosexual, lesbian and transgender agenda is not the only result of our gender rebellion as a nation. It is the most obvious, and it is the issue that typically rattles our dignity. But be assured that the ramifications of my own failure and disdain as a woman for the men in my life is not singularly my own. It echoes the moral sin of our nation and its influence has had dramatic impact on almost *every area of our lives.*

Mountain or molehill?

Just Exactly How Did We Get Here?

Is ignorance alone the root cause of our gender rebellion, as individual people and collectively, as a culture? If the church launched a "get-to-know-your-biblical-gender-design" campaign, would we have a chance at reclaiming God's glorious plan for men and women? (Can't you just imagine the bumper stickers?)

The bottom line is that biblical ignorance *is* an issue. We *do* need to discover the joy-filled, God-glorifying, hope-inspiring plan of the Creator for His people around this issue of gender. What *was* His plan? What has changed (if anything)? How does that impact our lives from one day to the next? What difference does it make in our relationships to our husbands? And what difference does it make to those of us who *don't have a husband*?

Those are valid questions and each is worthy of our careful study. In the pages that follow we will consider those questions and more as we look to Scripture and find the answers.

We will become well established in a biblical understanding of feminine godliness. We will be thinking women who know who God is and how He *really* means for us to live as women. Which is critical for our joy and His glory.

But information alone is never enough to *transform* lives and guarantee blessing. There is no formula: information + effort = godliness/happiness. Truthfully, this is so disappointing to me. I really just want you to tell me what to do. I can create a strategy. Make a list. Set some goals. I can do it.

That would work if I were, well, Jesus. The problem is not my effort. It's not my intention. It's not even my ignorance. It's my heart.

My heart, like the Israelites' of Jeremiah's day, is *desperately wicked.* On my best day, armed with biblical information and the best of intention, I worship at the altar of my own desires. My own agenda. My own comfort. Why did I not go back to Chas that evening, or the next day, to encourage him? It was not because of a lack of information. I *knew what was right.*

Ugh. The rebellion of my own desperately wicked heart.

The Genesis of Rebellion

Adam and Eve. Literally the perfect couple. They were uncorrupted and they were, together, fit for one another. Found in the early chapters of Genesis, things are so good that it would seem their story would end with the infamous words: "And they lived happily ever after."

But for the tree. And the fruit. And the serpent. (Cue the foreboding music.) Following the detailed account of creation in Genesis 1 and 2, Moses records a dialogue that took place between Eve and the serpent. The snake cozied up to the woman and spoke to her in a skillfully crafted riddle:

"Did God actually say *'You shall not eat of any tree in the garden'?"*[6]

No. God did not *actually* say that at all.

Without spending a great deal of time on this text, we need to acknowledge that, whatever else was going on, *Eve knew better*. Genesis 2:16 records God's actual command: *"You* ***may*** *surely eat of* ***every tree*** *of the garden, but of the* ***tree of the knowledge of good and evil*** you shall not eat." (Emphasis mine.) Nothing confusing about that.

Eve could not have forgotten God's explicit command. But the serpent's carefully chosen words caused her to question the benevolence of God.

Bible scholar James Montgomery Boice comments: "Satan suggests that God is not good, that He does not wish the very best of all worlds for His creatures."[7] Eve believed the serpent's sly "spin" on the Word of God. She bought into his lie.

And she ate. *"She took of its fruit and ate, and she also gave some to her husband who was with her, and he ate."*[8]

Much has been made about Eve's motivation for taking that fruit. For now, let's just acknowledge the obvious: Eve ate because she wanted to. God's instructions notwithstanding, Eve had a desire and she determined to fulfill it.

And so they sinned.

It may seem like a stretch, but this was the genesis of *my* rebellion. On that December evening I did not go back to my husband and try to encourage his leadership because I wanted

6 Genesis 3:1
7 *Genesis: An Expositional Commentary*, p. 135
8 Genesis 3:6

my own way. To go back felt awkward – and I wanted my own comfort. In some way, his withdrawal gave me a sense of superiority ("I can do this better anyway") – and I wanted my own agenda. It would have been humbling – and I wanted my own position.

Paul informs our thinking here. Adam's sin, Paul would say in Romans 5, became our sin. He represented the *whole human race* when he (in partnership with his bride) made the fateful decision to disobey the Creator of the Universe. "*Through one man, sin entered the world.*"[9]

Returning to our consideration of the current growing trend of women's disregard for men, how did we get here, both personally and corporately? How did we become so disdainful toward men? Where does our prideful independence come from? What causes our haughty condescension? What is the genesis of my wicked heart?

Our demand to have our own way, our refusal to live according to God's design for us as men and women, demonstrates the Romans 5 reality: through one man sin entered the world. Through one man, sin entered me. Jeremiah was right; every human being has a desperately wicked heart.

Information alone will not be enough to crush the rebellion that threatens us. We must acknowledge the ever-present reality of our sinful nature. We must be willing to look in the mirror and see ourselves as we really are: women who want to be satisfied. Acknowledged. Brilliant. Independent. *Free!* And we will do whatever it takes to secure these desires for ourselves.

Digging Deeper

My son and I have just finished putting in a small brick patio

9 Romans 5:12

in our front yard. What began with a simple idea to just "lay some bricks down" became a three-day, three-man-one-woman-and-a-baby project. Day one, Milas and I began to dig. We had done our research (thank you, DIY videos!) and we knew that we needed to dig down at least 8 inches. No problem. We pulled on our gloves, took our shovels in hand, and began to dig. We turned over an inch or so of dirt before the digging got, well, challenging.

What we did not take into consideration in our planning was the location of several *very large* trees in our general digging vicinity. Their roots extended into our digging area, and the root system was vast and sturdy. Within hours I was ready to throw in the towel and put what little dirt we had excavated back into the hole.

Underneath the soil of Eve's sin, her desire to have her own way, meet her own needs and gain her own freedom, Eve's deepest issue was her lack of faith in the God who had created her. Her unbelief was the stubborn root hidden under the surface of her faith and when she took that fruit, the root was exposed. Boice agrees: "This is the first revelation of sin's nature. *Sin is unbelief.* It is a rejection of God's good will and truthfulness, *leading inevitably to an act of outright rebellion.*"[10]

Didn't Eve know that God made her, that He understood her, loved her, and cared for her? This woman had everything – the perfect mate, a perfect home, and perfect communion with her Creator.

But it seems that in Eve's heart she was *already* questioning the character of God. She may have *said* that she believed that God loved her, that He had her best care in mind, that He gave her every good thing. But when presented with her own desire

10 *Genesis: An Expositional Commentary*, p. 135

having been withheld by God, she *didn't* really *believe in His goodness*. She was afraid that she was missing out on something and concluded that she must take matters into her own hands.

Did Eve make a wrong decision? Indeed she did. Was she taking responsibility that was not hers, being pushy and manipulative? Indeed she was, and her decision had an unfathomable impact on all of history. Believe me, we'll come back to that. For now, we must acknowledge that the issue equally significant to her *rebellion* was the reason behind her sin – the *disconnect between what Eve* knew *and what she actually believed.* Her practical unbelief.

How did we get here? We have an "information problem." And, according to Romans 5, we have a "sin problem." But at our core, we have a "faith problem."

Every temptation to sin has as its heartbeat the matter of faith. In every case, our sin is an act of defiance against the character of God. We sin because we do not believe *something* about Him. We are no different from our first parents. Transformation of my desperately wicked heart to one that is like Christ *does* require that I do battle with my sin. But what I *do* depends completely and wholly on what I *believe* to be true about God. In the early years of my marriage, if I had *believed God* for Hannah's future spiritual benefit, I may have encouraged Chas to be her spiritual leader, even if he would do things differently than I would. If I had *trusted God's sovereign plan* for my life, I would have submitted to the leadership of my husband – even though it was *really hard.*

Obedience on the outside – submission, respect, a gentle and quiet spirit – is not only impossible in the long term, whatever "success" is achieved is rubbish unless it flows from faith in the Eternal Covenant-Keeping God.

Sisters, information *is* important. We will spend the remaining chapters of this book discovering what Scripture says about God's plan for women. We need to be *rightly informed.* In addition, we will look into the mirror to discover the patterns of sin that remain in our lives so that we may repent and experience the Spirit's power to change us.

But before we go forward, we must acknowledge the mountain of unbelief that threatens us. What we *know* is too often not connected to *how we live.* We must learn that *our* choices flow not out of our knowledge of what to do, but out of our knowledge of God *and our trust in Him.* Eve knew that God loved her, but she *questioned* His love for her in that moment – and her lack of trust informed her actions.

If we really believe that God is Lord and King, that He is all-knowing, that He is powerful and that He loves us with an everlasting love, then we are able to live in a manner that reflects such faith. We can take risks (aka "submit"). We can defer to others (aka "respect"). We can practice contentment (aka "gentle and quiet"). We can serve others. We can sacrifice our own wills. Not because we are trying to earn His favor, but because we trust His character and nature.

A Mountain of Ignorance – and Sin – and Unbelief

Are you beginning to see that what presented itself as a molehill – my wrong choice in an awkward moment – was, in reality, a mountain of ignorance, wickedness (sin) and unbelief? I had not only an "informational" gap about godly womanhood – but the gap between what I have known *about* God for all of my life and how that knowing should impact my choices, my thoughts, my words and my relationships had not yet taken root in my heart and mind. If you had asked me, I would have told you that I loved and trusted Him (remember, I was on staff at my church!). *Practically,* my life did not reflect such faith. And, like Eve, too often my sinful desires ruled my soul.

And everyone has suffered. Both of my children. My gracious husband. And me. Each member of my little family has been impacted by my sin and faithlessness. Even though I didn't mean for it to happen.

Here's the good news: God is sufficient for the mountain of my sin and unbelief. That's the "happy ending" found in Genesis 3. We'll get into this more in a later chapter, but notice for now the *promise* and *hope* that God pronounces as Adam and his bride leave the garden: *"He shall bruise your head and you shall bruise his heel."*[11] It may seem obscure, but this is actually the first pronouncement of the Gospel! This hope, the defeat of the enemy, ultimately comes to fulfillment in Christ. All of the chaos in our lives personally and corporately in the world will be made right on that day.

In the meantime, and because of Jesus, God has richly blessed both my marriage and our family. What is amazing to me is that God has given Chas and me such an affection for one another and He has preserved our family *in spite of my sin.*

What a stunning example of God's covenant love! My persistent waywardness as a woman and a wife does not compromise His steadfast love. Though I have been faithless, God remains faithful still.

It is this steady, persistent refusal of God to wash His hands of me that has left me desperate to understand *His* plan for me as a woman and as a wife. If, in His steadfast love for me, God has a plan for my good that informs my life as a woman with

11 Genesis 3:15

Chas, and with the children, and (by the way) with the rest of my family, my coworkers and my neighbors, *how can I know what it is,* and *how can I grow in my capacity to live in light of what I believe?*

Three Steps to Godly Womanhood. Or maybe Five.

The danger, now, is for me to launch into "fix it" mode. What to do? Or, probably more to the point, what *not* to do? As a woman of faith, a Christ-follower, a lover of the church, what can *I do* to be more godly? To stay out of the shadow of this frightening, overwhelming, threatening mountain? To *undo* the damage that has resonated in our family for two decades? To have an impact on the world around me?

I wish I could articulate what needs to be said here in a three-step plan. Honestly, I could sell a lot of books; I looked. Amazon.com carries these titles:

"Three steps to a Strong Family"

"Three steps to mastery of Bruce Lee"

"Three steps to Incredible Health"

"Three Steps to Enlightenment"

If you're willing to go a few extra steps, you can have forgiveness, romantic love, and AP Psychology in *five* steps.

Sisters, this is not going to be a book about "Three steps to Godly Womanhood." It is not a handbook. This issue is, obviously, too entrenched for an easy fix.

On the pages that follow, we'll address **the information gap** – focusing on gaining a solid, theologically sound foundation for understanding God's design for women. It is true that information alone will not save us, but we cannot be saved from our rebellion without right, biblical thinking.

Secondly, we need to become **skilled and disciplined repenters** – which will lead us from our sin to obedience. We must begin to seek the Lord and ask Him to *reveal our sin,* protecting us from the temptation to live independently from Him. We need to be quick to recognize our well-worn habits of disrespect, disdain, and contempt – toward men, toward women and toward God and we must acknowledge our need for mercy. And then we must *obey.*

Finally, much of the text that follows will **focus on our faith**. What we believe from Scripture and from history about God – our practical theology – will be the power for real and lasting change, for sanctifying transformation that reflects Christ and brings ultimate glory to the Father. Do we *really* believe that God is sovereign, that He is just, that He is good, that He will *take care of us?* Will we accept the plan that He has for our lives – as women – believing that *it is good,* even if it is hard?

Sarah Hoped in God

In the context of his discourse on godly wives, Peter connects this issue of *gender* with *faith* and *obedience* as he calls to mind the faithfulness of God by commending Sarah's story. (Single friends, hang on…this applies to you! I know this because the word "women" in the following verse is translated in the Greek Lexicon as "a woman of any age, whether a virgin, or married or a widow.")

"For this is how the holy women who hoped in God *used to adorn themselves, by submitting to their own husbands, as Sarah obeyed Abraham, calling him lord. And you are her children, if you do good and do not fear anything that is frightening"* (1 Peter 3:5, 6).

Sarah hoped in God.

She submitted to her husband and obeyed him.

She did good and did not fear anything that was frightening.

One occasion of Sarah's obedience is told in the early chapters of Genesis. The Lord instructed Abraham to leave his home and move to a new country. In the course of this journey, God revealed His covenant promise to Abraham: "I will be your God and you will be my people" (Genesis 15). Additionally, it was during this time that God promised Abraham and Sarah a son (Genesis 18).

However, even in the context of God's tangible presence, twice while on this journey through foreign lands Abraham[12] felt afraid, threatened by the local rulers. He came up with a plan, asking Sarah to pose as his sister, so that the King, taken by her beauty, would not murder Abraham as a means to have Sarah as his Queen-Bride.

Sarah did as Abraham asked. However, his plan went awry as Sarah was taken into the harem of the king. Pause and think about how *frightening* this prospect would have been for Sarah. How was she able to do such a thing?

This is Peter's point. It is not the greatness of Sarah that he lauds. It is the greatness of God – His plan, and His promise. Peter helps us see that Sarah's *theology* informed her life! She *remembered* the covenant-keeping God. Don't miss Peter's description: **Sarah hoped in God**. She *did not fear anything that was frightening* because she was able to hang on to what she knew was true about God. He had been faithful. He was sufficient, even as she was taken into the king's harem.

Can you imagine the risk?

12 For simplicity, I am using the names "Abraham and Sarah", even though the first occasion of this sin took place before the Lord changed their names (Genesis 12).

God was faithful and He kept His promise. He protected Sarah. He preserved her marriage to Abraham, and, as such, He saved the promised seed that was to lead to the coming of Christ!

I know there are *lots* of questions that come up when we consider this story, but focus on *Peter's* exhortation. We know that it was God's plan (His design) and His present protection that sustained Sarah when Abraham failed her. It was the work of God that allowed Sarah to *"hope in [Him],"* to *"not fear anything that was frightening."* It was God's covenant faithfulness – "I will be your God and you will be my people" – that kept Sarah safe as she lived in the context of her *design* and God's *promise.*

All of our modern, ethical questions about whether Sarah should have obeyed Abraham's seemingly outrageous request[13] should pale in comparison to this: GOD IS FAITHFUL. This occasion of God's faithfulness to Sarah illustrates her loving obedience as an overflow of her *theology,* her practical faith. Whatever Sarah's understanding of God's design for her, she must have exercised the discipline to believe that His plan was best and to *act accordingly.* Most significantly, she *trusted the character of God,* choosing to obey because she knew that He would protect her and preserve her because He had made this little family a promise!

As we consider this story, we ought to gain confidence in the nature and character and promises of God for us *as women.* Our trust is in the Lord – He is sovereign. He has a plan for us. He will never leave us. *He never fails.* This is the **theology** that

13 It is important that the reader not conclude from this one story that wives should submit to husbands' sinful, outrageous demands. Abraham and Sarah lived in a different culture, in a different time in the life of God's people. They did not have, for instance, the indwelling presence of the Holy Spirit. They did not have the benefit of a church family. This circumstance is highly unusual and should be considered in its own context. If a wife finds herself in a parallel situation in our contemporary culture, she must get counsel from her elders and pastors before determining a course of action.

informs my every choice *as a woman*. It is *thinking* theology, but it is also *practical!* It inspires my faith and fuels my obedience.

Molehill or Mountain – What's the Verdict?

So what's the verdict? Does my failure in that fateful moment with Chas and Hannah look like a molehill or mountain? How about our collective gender rebellion as a nation? Molehill? Mountain?

Information is important. Our perspective of womanhood has been influenced more by the culture and by our own agenda than by God's Word. We have drifted from His design so dramatically that it will be challenging to reorient our thinking. Recovering the biblical framework for womanhood is not for the faint of heart.

But you know by now that information alone will not save us. We must examine ourselves and deal with our sin. We must consider what we know to be true about God from Scripture. We must ask the Holy Spirit to reveal our own hearts so that we may see the disconnect between what we know to be true about God and our *practical theology* – that is, how we live.

The distance between our faith and our actual lives is not insurmountable, but it's not a molehill either. The decision to face the mountain is one that has opportunity for dramatic impact not only on our lives, but also on our families, the church, and the world.

These pages have, perhaps, been very discouraging. It does, indeed, seem that we are standing in the shadow of Mount Everest. As I recall my own history and culpability, I can be easily defeated. I sometimes wonder what God might have done had I exercised my faith in His gracious plan for me as a bride.

What if I had believed in God's good plan and trusted Him, gone back to Chas that evening and encouraged him? Had I apologized and affirmed the effort that he was making? Had I gently insisted the next evening that we try again? Had I been humble and gracious, instead of awkward and dismissive, what might God have done in my husband? In me? In our children? What heartache might we have avoided?

Earth Movers

Much of this chapter has been a recounting of my story. My journey from sinful rebellion is not over, but I am grateful, as I look back, to see God's mercy and grace. He is steadfast and faithful as His Spirit transforms me into the image of His Son[14], which is ultimately His good plan for all of my life this side of heaven. It is this *transforming work* that brings God great glory, and gives me true joy.

So you already know about me. Perhaps the pages that follow will stir up *your* soul around godly womanhood as we consider together the Creator's good plan for women from the beginning. What might God be calling you to *be* and to *do* in light of the Truth that you find in these pages?

Accurate, biblical information is necessary for the Spirit's work of transformation – and you will get plenty of that between the covers of this book. However, addressing the issues of sin and unbelief will be between you and the Father. Repentance and faith. These are gifts from God alone.

Many centuries after Sarah and Abraham's dramatic story, Jesus would say to His disciples:

"For truly, I say to you, if you ***have faith like a grain of mustard***

14 2 Corinthians 3:18

***seed**, you will say to this **mountain**, 'Move from here to there,' and it will move, and nothing will be impossible for you"* (Matthew 17:20).

Before you go forward, ask God to give you faith like a grain of mustard seed to move the mountain of ignorance, sin and unbelief in your own soul. Then hang onto your hat and read on. Let's "*move from here to there*" together, shall we?

Chapter Two

THREE PRINCIPLES FROM THE GARDEN

My good friend Tracy has volunteered as a buddy for children in the Bronx for several years. One day, she opened her storybook Bible to read to the children about the creation. She showed her little audience the colorful picture of Adam and Eve and asked: "Do you know who these people are?" One little boy proudly replied: "Tarzan and Jane!"

Well, close.

The words of Genesis 1, obviously better known to some than to others, read:

"Let us make man in our image, after our likeness. So God created man in His own image, in the image of God He created him; male and female He created them" (Genesis 1:26, 1:27).

This text will become very familiar, as it is the basis for our broad understanding of what it means to be created by God with a *uniquely feminine* design (aka "Jane"). If we've grown up in the church and we're accustomed to the text of the Genesis account, the temptation is to see nothing new or interesting and quickly move on to the next chapter. But let's linger here for just a moment.

These 31 words may appear inoffensive and harmless. However, these phrases from the pen of Moses introduce concepts and principles that have recently been hotly debated not by the secular community, but by those of us in the evangelical church. The topic is so "hot" that few pastors are willing to address the issue of biblical manhood and womanhood because the risk is too great and the audience too hostile.[15]

Yet it seems wise to look carefully at the text and put forth a few fundamental principles. These will undergird our consideration of what we know about God and how that relates to womanhood. Reputable authors have written *volumes* on these issues, and these are well worth the read.[16] Here, for the sake of brevity we will focus on a few basic principles about God, a theological framework that will help us to understand the text and should inform our discussion.

God created all people, men and women, in His image.

God created all people, men and women, *equal* in His image; equal does not mean "same."

God created men and women to be different in ways that were designed for His glory and for our good *at the time of creation.*

These principles, clearly set forth in the familiar story of creation, are affirmed – like a thread woven in a tapestry – throughout all of Scripture. However, like a well-told family story, the details have been neglected from overuse, and we have forgotten the import of Moses' chronicle of our very beginning. Let's look carefully at a few astonishing details.

Principle #1: God created all people, men and women, in His image.

"Let us make man in our image." What exactly does that mean?

Not all commentators and theologians agree on the response.

15 http://cbmw.org/uncategorized/jbmw-forum-q-a-on-the-local-church/
16 Wayne Grudem, Dan Doriani, John Piper, Mike Ross, Ray Ortlund, John Frame, Susan Hunt and Elyse Fitzpatrick to name a few.

Nevertheless there are several explanations that would gain consensus with most Bible thinkers. We'll focus on those agreeable points, as they are enough to make the case that our having been made in the image of God is paramount to our understanding of His plan for our lives.

First, it is important to acknowledge that being made *in the image of God* means that man, as a creation, is unique. He is not, as purported by some contemporary thinkers, like the animals but better.[17] He is not a more sophisticated, highly developed species of mammal. He is different. Special.

Notice that before the creation of mankind, Moses describes God's creation of all the other living things on the earth as having been created *"according to* their *kinds."* That phrase is used four times in verses 24 and 25. But of humanity, God said, "*Let us make man in* our *image* [according to *our* 'kind']." A forum of reformed authors describes this important nuance: "Our real significance is found in our identity as creatures specially made by God in his image and likeness. This is our glory and the source of our true dignity."[18] By God's design, we are *not at all like the animals,* made according to *their kind.* We are different. Unique. Special. *In His image.*

Genesis 5 is an account of Adam's family lineage. In verses 1-3, Moses describes the Adam family (smile) this way: "*When Adam had lived 130 years he fathered a son* in his own likeness, after his image, *and named him Seth."* See what he's saying? Adam had a son who *was like him.*

I have three brothers. This discussion only involves two, because the third is adopted. But that's the point. Of the three, my dad's two sons *bear his resemblance.* My third brother, while

17 http://phys.org/news/2013-12-humans-smarter-animals-experts.html
18 SBJT, p. 82

equally loved and cherished, does not carry my dad's DNA. He does not *bear his image*. Each of the other boys, however, bears a striking resemblance to my dad. Since my dad went home to be with the Lord, his image bearing through them is eerily familiar. It's almost like when they are both in the room, much of my dad is in the room with them.

As Seth was made *in the likeness* of Adam, and Doug and Josh were made *in the likeness* of my dad, we are made *in the likeness* of our Heavenly Father. He has created us with certain attributes that are *like Him*. We actually *resemble Him*. We are made in His image.

But what does it mean to *bear God's image*?

What Exactly Is "His Likeness?"

Every child in every Sunday School class for generations has learned the series of creation days, from Day One's "light and darkness" to "the beasts of the earth" on Day Six.

As Moses describes this astounding scene, he notes that every act of creation is initiated merely by God's spoken command. The words: *"And God said, let there be…"* are repeated seven times in twenty-four verses. Every occasion of the repeated phrase is a command. *God said, let there be…* AND IT WAS.

Notice now a small detail from verse 26 that sets this act of creation apart from the others: *"Then God said, 'Let* us *make man in* our *image, after* **our** *likeness…"*

Do you see it? There is a subtle, but significant, shift in God's creative MO. This is not a command "let there be." It is a dialogue. A consultation. Among parties.

Hmm mm… This is the very first time we see the occasion of the plural personal pronouns: us, our. And that's not just grammatically significant. It reveals something about the nature of God that is noteworthy for our continued consideration. God exists in *community*, three-in-one. Father, Son and Spirit – The Trinity. He has created us in His image with the same instinct for relationship. We need each other. God has stamped His image on us as *relational beings.*

Additionally, commentators agree that being made *in the image of God* means that we are endowed with the capacity for and the responsibility to rule. The "ruler" image of God is established throughout this creation account as He ordains and executes His own plan for each and every stage of the creative process. His authoritative voice breathes into existence something from nothing. Verse 28 reveals this authority aspect of the image of God in His human creation as He urges Adam and Eve to *"fill the earth* ***and subdue it.****"* Such a command is not given to any other created being. It is only in humanity that God has endowed the intellectual and moral capacity to rule. In this way, as "rulers," His image has been woven into ours.

One final example of our *image bearing* of our Creator is that we are endowed with an immortal, spiritual aspect to our existence. The very first verse of Scripture gives us a clue about God with the words *"In the beginning, God…"* Before the world began, before time and space even existed, God was there. The breath of God did not begin at the time of creation. It has *always been.* We describe this as God's eternality. He has always existed. He always will exist.

The Genesis 2 account of God's creation of humanity ascribes a facet of His eternality to this unique being. It is an important distinction between God's creation of people and that of every other creature: *"The Lord God formed man of dust from the ground, and breathed into his nostrils the breath of life; and man became a living being."* Breathed into his nostrils the breath of life. That "breath of God" birthed within Adam a soul, a spirit. He became not just a man, but also a *spiritual being*. One whose life actually goes on *forever.*[19] No other creature has such a soul. The image of God is reflected in our eternal spirit. No other creation has been given such a gift!

God exists in plurality, in community. As image-bearers, we live in community with others.

God exercises authority. As image-bearers, He has given us the capacity and responsibility to "rule."

God is eternal. As image-bearers, we are spiritual, eternal beings.

God's design for our image-bearing is surely not limited to these few applications. Indeed, they are meant to demonstrate a much larger, much deeper theology than is possible to plumb here. For our purposes, we want to see that this "glory of God which peculiarly shines forth in human nature"[20] is at the very core of our understanding of human life in general and our feminine identity in particular. We must begin here if we are going to have a sound, biblical view of "womanhood." What we learn in these verses is that it was God's plan and design to create us to *resemble* Him. Men and women, we "*bear His image*" as human beings. This is not an insignificant detail but, rather, a foundational principle to all of life and faith.

God created all people, men and women, in His image.

Principle #2: God created all people, men and women, *equal* in His image.

The church has not always been at the forefront of social

19 John 3:16; Romans 6:23
20 John Calvin

issues. It is true, and to our shame, that we did not always lead the fight against slavery, we often failed to champion the disenfranchised, and we have been known to trample the dignity of women. At the core of such injustice is a misunderstanding of this important theological principle: *God created all people, men and women, equal in His image.*

Equal in the image of God. Equal in importance to Him. Equal in personhood. Equal in worth before Him.

Any discussion of gender that has Scripture as its foundation must begin with this truth. God created men and women equally in His image.

"So God created man in his own image, in the image of God he created him; male and female he created them." [21]

From the very beginning, at the moment of the Trinitarian consultation about humanity, God planned for His image-bearing in both the male and female creation *equally.* In the Bible, this verse is often inset into the margin, setting it apart as if it is very important. We are not to miss this. God created all people, men and women, equal in His image.

The New Testament offers further evidence of our equality in our image-bearing and value. It is to both men and women that the Holy Spirit is given.[22] Baptism is offered to men and women,[23] as is church membership. Spiritual gifts are given to both men and women equally.[24] Finally, the Apostle Paul warns the church about factions based on external factors, and he includes gender in that list.[25]

The male dominance and pride that have been seen in nearly

21 Genesis 1:27
22 Acts 2:17-18
23 Acts 2:41
24 1 Corinthians 12:7; Ephesians 4:7
25 Galatians 3:28

all cultures in history is not by God's design, but is instead a result of the fall of man described in chapter 3 of Genesis. One author has stated that male domination is not a Biblical doctrine but a personal moral failure.[26] The male superiority, dominance, and abuse that have plagued our nation's history are not and never have been the character and nature of God's design for gender. Such thinking is a result of sin and to promote it is to deny the biblical truth of equality in the image of God.

Because God created us *together* in His image, men and women can be assured that we are equally important to God. The idea that men are more valuable to Him and that women are somehow inferior is unequivocally unbiblical. The church *must* set the pace here. We must promote the value of all of God's people irrespective of gender, race, heritage, or socio-economic status. Wayne Grudem, in his important work *Biblical Foundations for Manhood and Womanhood*,[27] puts it this way: "Men and women share equally in the tremendous privilege of being in the image of God."

Whatever we do, in whatever direction our thinking leads, we must not ignore this truth: God created all people, men and women, equal in His image. Equal as image-bearers. Equal in personhood. Equal in value.

We, men and women, are image-bearing twins. Can I get an "Amen"?

However

However, ***equal does not mean "same."***

The American Heritage Dictionary defines "equal" as "having the same quantity, measure, or value as another. Being the

26 *Male and Female Equality and Male Headship*, Raymond C. Ortlund
27 *Biblical Foundations for Manhood and Womanhood*, p. 20

same or identical to *in value*. Having the same privileges, status, or rights." This definition does not indicate that "equal equals same."

Even children understand that "equal does not mean same." We learn early on that four quarters are equal to one dollar, but they are not the same. The quarters are round, and silver, and made of metal. The dollar is green. It is made of paper. They are *equal*. But not *the same*.

Chas and I have two children. We love them equally and they have the *same value* in our hearts and minds. We applied the same principles to both the children as we raised them, but they are not at all the same. NOT AT ALL. Hannah is an introvert and is most comfortable among her friends and family. Milas is an extrovert – happiest when he is in a crowd. Hannah is enthusiastic, vibrant, and intense. Milas is thoughtful, introspective, and verbose. They are not the same. But they are equal in status and position in our family.

One cup of water is equal in measure to one cup of flour. But they are not the same.

One small spoonful of peanut butter is equal in calories to a whole plate of broccoli. But they are clearly not the same.

To presume *sameness* in the name of *equality* doesn't make sense, even from a purely practical perspective.

This translation of "equal means same" has crept into our theology from our culture. John Piper warns, "Our culture is pressing us on almost every side to discount this reality [of gender distinction] and think of ourselves and each other merely in terms of a set of impersonal competencies and gender-blind personality traits."[28]

28 *For Single Men & Women*, p. 14

Piper's words, written more than twenty years ago, were sadly prophetic. Surely Dr. Piper could not have anticipated the trend toward gender-neutral accommodations in schools, retail businesses and offices, the removal of "labels" from children's toys to disassociate them from gender[29] and ultimately, the legalization of same-sex marriage. Families are avoiding gender stereotypes as they rear their children, hoping to avoid "pigeonholing" them in their formative years of development as "male" or "female." As a culture we are moving toward making no distinction at all between the sexes.

Pressed on every side.

It is true that our nation and our churches have a *history* of dismissing whole populations of people – image bearers of the Creator. We have a sense of desperate responsibility to *over-correct* the errors of our forefathers. For centuries women have endured the disdain and dismissal of men, so we are passionate to affirm our equality. And that is understandable.

But promoting *sameness*, becoming "gender blind" is not the answer. It's actually not even possible. What is happening in our families, and our churches and our neighborhoods is the acceptance of a "new normal" that is distinctly unbiblical. According to Genesis 1, we are not free to "determine our own identities." The text instructs us – and all of Scripture affirms – that God created us equally in His image. We bear His image equally. We are equal in personhood. Equal in value. But "equal" is not in opposition to "different."

In all likelihood, you are agreeing with me. But what is significant for today's Christian woman is – even as we collectively sigh at these notions as if we are disappointed in the thinking

29 *The Los Angeles Times*, "Target plays catch-up in removing gender-based toy labels," 11/14/15

of others – that we begin to see that in very subtle and insidious ways we are capitulating to this tragic thinking.

Principle #3: Men and women are different in ways that were designed by God at the time of creation.

The dismissal of "gender personhood" is a great and tragic loss. To presume *sameness* in the name of equality does no one any favors. It does not promote freedom. It does not ensure success. Rather, such thinking is taking a toll on generations of young people who do not understand or appreciate the import of what it means to be a man or a woman.

Gender distinctives may not be "erased" by man because they are not *erasable*. They are created into us *as image bearers of God*. The Danvers Statement, published by the Council on Biblical Manhood and Womanhood, makes this bold statement: "Distinctions in masculine and feminine roles are ordained by God as part of the created order and should find an echo in every human heart."

Let's return to the text in Genesis to consider the creation account as a means to rediscover the distinctions ordained by God. Having told the creation story in chapter 1 in its entirety, Moses goes back to provide detail and color to God's creation of *people* in chapter 2. While the creation account in Genesis 1 offers a broad chronological outline of the events of the creation week, Moses concentrates on creation's climax in chapter 2: the origin of mankind made in the very image of God. Here, Moses sets his focus on Adam, giving special import to God's plan for man, the preparation of his home and the "genesis" of his family.

As I've studied these verses in the context of social issues before us today, however, I wonder if chapter 2 is also important as a means to help us clarify some of the confusion around gender. Perhaps the details in chapter 2 were significant in Moses' spirit-filled mind at least partially because of the very questions that are being raised in our generation. In any case, we must not miss these details.

Yes, Adam Was Created First

As obvious as it may seem, the temporal order (the timing) of the creation of humanity as male and then female is significant. Genesis 2:7 describes Adam's creation. Eve does not come into the picture until verse 21. This begs the question; "If God intended His created beings to be exactly the same, why did He not create them *at the same time*? Like twins?"

The fact that God created Adam first and then Eve has significant theological meaning beyond the principle of general difference, as it gave the man the position of headship. I know this may cause the hair on the back of your neck to raise just a bit, but this idea of order at the time of creation reflects the heart of God for His people, and, as such, it sets an important biblical precedent. Paul affirms this nuance when he writes to Timothy in 1 Timothy 2:13. He cites the fact that *"Adam was formed first, then Eve"* as a reason for men and women having different roles in the New Testament church.

It is not my intent, and I do not have the space, to elaborate on this idea of male headship and authority here. There are biblical texts that address this doctrine very clearly and I would commend those texts for your further study.[30]

The point is that it is at least worth some thought to explore *why* God created man first and then woman? We believe that

30 Ephesians 5:21-33; Colossians 3:18-19; 1 Peter 3:1-7; Titus 2:5; 1 Timothy 3:4, 12; Genesis 1-3

God never does anything indiscriminately. Every single act of the Godhead is scripted for a purpose. It seems, then, that this order of creation was intended to make clear some aspect of the *distinction* between male and female. God was demonstrating an invisible reality by providing a visible, tangible reference point.

Interestingly, we know that Adam and his bride were both created on the sixth day. We don't know how much time elapsed between the "birth" of Adam and God's creation of Eve, but we *do* know that several things happened between the two events. Moses records a conversation between God and Adam in Genesis 2:16, 17. He elaborates on Adam's responsibility to name the animals, a task that took place while Adam was still alone. We know that Adam took a really good nap described by Moses as a "deep sleep."

And *then* there was Eve. The time lapse. It's one way in which they are *different.*

God intentionally created Adam first; then Eve. This was not an afterthought, but a strategic and purposeful part of His plan.

We may not like its implications. But this detail informs our faith, and begins our serious discussion about gender distinction as a part of creation.

The Dust and the Rib

In Genesis 2:7, Moses uses an economy of words to describe an epic occasion. God formed Adam from the dust of the ground.

I happen to be writing this chapter while at the beach, and as I consider this "forming from the dust" I am thinking of all of the structures that my children have "formed from the sand" over the years. While their efforts have been fairly elementary (although this year the boys constructed an entire putt-putt course!), I've seen pictures of very elaborate and intricate creations that people have formed from the sand. Lifelike sea creatures, complex castles, and sophisticated replicas of cultural icons can be carefully constructed by gifted people (with lots of time on their hands). So I can, in my sanctified imagination, at least consider what this "forming from the dust" may have looked like.

But then…

"The Lord God…breathed into his nostrils the breath of life."[31] God breathed life into his nostrils. God Himself breathed life in the nostrils of this new creature. Have you ever considered that every being created before this moment, all the "*great sea creatures*" and "*every living creature that moves, with which the waters swarm*" and every "*winged bird*" and the "*livestock and creeping things and beasts of the earth*", each of these was *given* life by the Creator. But for this new creation, God Himself breathed life into his nostrils. Wow.

Then, after a series of events, God created woman.

"So the Lord God caused a deep sleep to fall upon the man, and while he slept took one of his ribs and closed up its place with flesh. And the rib that the Lord God had taken from the man he made into a woman."[32]

God took the man that He fashioned from the dust and put him to sleep. While he was sleeping, the Creator removed a rib from the man and, from the rib, He made a woman. Once more, the wonder of such a statement tends to elude us because we've read it so many times. God took a rib from the man, closed up his flesh, and used the rib to make a woman. How absolutely

31 Genesis 2:7
32 Genesis 2:21

stunning and marvelous and amazing.

Superlatives aside, this question remains: after sculpting the man from the dust of the ground, and breathing life into him, why did God not take more of the same dust to form the woman? God could have created them, each of them, in the same manner, but He didn't. Why?

There is (again) deep theological meaning to the manner in which God created Adam and Eve, but for our purposes it is enough to *notice* that God used a different means to create each. God used a different *means* to create them because they *are* different.

The Design Itself

Did you know that, on average:

- Men weigh 15% more than women?
- Men are taller than women by about 6 inches?
- Men have more total muscle mass than women?
- Men have a more pronounced Adam's apple due to larger vocal chords? (Which explains the low voice.)
- Male skin is thicker than female?

It is likely that none of those details are a surprise to you. But have you ever wondered *why* there are these differences? Do you think God just got bored with Adam and He wanted to try His creative hand at something new?

Our differences even in structure and design have rich implications, but for now it's enough to acknowledge that men and women *look different*. In many ways, we are different from the inside out.

God created Adam and Eve at different times.

He created them using different means.

He created each with a unique physical design. From the very beginning.

God created us equally in His image; but equal does not mean "same." Men and women are different in ways that were designed by God at the time of creation.

But I want to push this thinking just a little further, because God's plan for our uniqueness – by design – is not limited to our appearance, or even to our internal structure. To a certain degree, the differences that we've discovered are indicators of something more. Scripture gives us a couple of clues that reveal God's further unique plan for each of His children, male and female.

Something Is Not right

Returning to the creation account in Genesis 1, the phrase "*It was good*" is repeated in verses 4, 10, 12, 18 and 25. Then, in verse 31, to capture the *entire* creation (including man and woman), God employs the remarkable *"Behold, it was very good."*

Let's look at the details, Moses' "color commentary" in chapter 2. Verse 18 is the first indicator that something was not right. *"Then the Lord God said, 'It is not good that the man should be alone.'"* It is important to acknowledge here that God did not just discover that Adam was alone. He did not forget, or overlook a detail, or make a mistake. The musing of the Lord God recorded out loud for us by Moses was not His wondering what to do. It was His *letting us in on* a great cosmic plan that would have deep and powerful significance for the human race throughout history. It was NEVER part of God's creation plan for man to be alone…He just wanted us to see how *not good* that option would be. This was part of His plan from the very beginning. He's just declaring here that He is not finished yet. It is not good that Adam is alone.

So God sends the animals. Man's best friends.

One by one God *"brought them to the man"* and Adam had the distinct privilege of naming each one. Can you just imagine what he was thinking? Every creature, so familiar to us, was new and strange and amazing to the first Adam! Hit "pause" for just a moment. Picture Adam, pacing back and forth as the animals go by, expressing his surprise and pleasure at each odd character (like the octopus – how did God *bring the octopus* to Adam? Again – hmm mm). But something is missing.

You have to wonder: Does Adam look at these creatures and *not* notice that there are at least *two* of each?. Every creature is part of a "pack," or a "school," or a "colony," or a "gaggle." (Seriously. That's many geese in one group. It's a gaggle.) Many lions. Many moose. Many ants.

One Adam.

Of *course* Adam noticed. Verse 20 tells us *"But for Adam there was not found a helper fit for him."* Sad.

If God knew that it would not be good for Adam to be alone, why did He leave Him alone for some time? Remember that this was not an oversight, or afterthought. It was part of the plan *from the beginning.* We've already suggested that at least one reason God created Adam *first* was to establish an important difference between the man and the woman. But I wonder if He allowed Adam to go through this *looking for a companion* so that he would *see his need*?

Something is missing when man is alone. SOMETHING IS MISSING! Adam's uniqueness was insufficient. All of those differences that we cited (and more) were not enough to sustain him, even in the garden of perfection.

Here It Comes

Adam looked. *"But for Adam there was not found a* helper fit for him." Notice the similarity of Adam's discovery to God's thinking from verse 18, *"It is not good that the man should be alone; I will make a* helper fit for him."

What was Adam looking for? He was not looking for a companion. Or a lover. Or a soul mate – a partner – a friend. By God's design and in His image, Adam was looking for a *helper* who would *fit him*.

Sisters, don't roll your eyes. I know what you are thinking. I've shared this truth with many women in various settings and their reaction is fairly predictable. While no one has actually said this, here's what I suspect is going on in her mind:

"A HELPER?!? Are you *kidding me*? Of course he wants a *helper*. Every man I've ever known wants a *helper*. So **this** is how that started?"

Yes, friend. Every man you have ever known wants a helper. And this *is* how that started.

Let me remind you of a few important details that are easily overlooked in our outrage at such a turn of events.

First, this moment in time takes place in the garden *before the fall.* Remember that Adam and Eve were *uncorrupted* before the fall. There is *no sin* in Adam. None. Not one selfish, egotistical, domineering thought or motive. Created, by the way, in *God's image*. The God who is fair, good, loving, and wise. So it is very important to know that this need for a *helper* was an expression of his perfect image-bearing personhood. He *really did need a helper.* This was not Adam's self-obsessed need-based hunt for a good-looking servant. God created Adam with a "perfect" need. For a helper.

Second, at the risk of being redundant, there is a reason that

God did not create Adam and Eve *at the same time*. It was in God's plan for Adam to *recognize* his need. God expected Adam to notice the gap. He knew that it would be important for Adam to experience being "alone" so that he would know that it was *not good*. Are you beginning to see why this is important for our generation? How many men – and women – do you know who are abandoning their marriages because they think they are better off *on their own*?

Third, it was important for Adam not just to see a gap, but also to see *exactly what his need was*. Exactly. Adam needed to see his bride as *exactly what he needed*. He was not looking for a full and happy life. He was not looking for the girl of his dreams. He was not even "looking for love." That's what *we've* made of this story. We've turned the story of Adam and Eve into a modern-day romance that is paltry in comparison to God's design. God planned for Adam to look for exactly what he needed.

A helper. One that was *"fit for him."*

The "H" Word

The Hebrew text here can be translated literally as *"I will make* for him *a helper fit for him."* Paul writes in 1 Corinthians 11: *"For indeed man was not created for the woman's sake but woman for the man's sake."* Paul was not being chauvinistic or demeaning of women. He was exercising his theology. Wayne Grudem has written "Genesis 2 does not merely say that Eve *functions* as Adam's helper in one or two specific events. Rather, it says that God made Eve for the purpose of providing Adam with help, one who *by virtue of creation* would function as Adam's 'helper'."[33]

33 *Recovering Biblical Manhood and Womanhood*

I am aware that this thinking makes women squirm. It makes me squirm. But this is what Scripture says, and God's Word applies no matter what circumstances may define your life at this moment. *"I will make a helper fit for him"* is one of the most definitive statements by God – not about our *value*, but about our *design*.

Remember where we began. The first two principles of our discussion:

God created all people, men and women, in His image.

God created all people, men and women, equal in His image. Equal does not mean "same."

This idea of being made a "helper fit for him" does not negate either principle. God designed the helper as a person equally significant in His image, as is the man, for whom she is fit. Has she been treated as inferior? Indeed. In the culture, in history, and in the church.

But we must remember that errors of male dominance and male superiority (and, by the way, feminine manipulation and disdain) have come as the result of faithlessness and sin. This is why it is so important to hang on to these principles. At the *very beginning of God's Word*, a mere twenty-seven verses into what would become sixty-six books, the Holy Spirit declares the truth that has become an essential, undeniable witness against the threat of oppression: *"in the image of God He created him; male and female He created them ... I will make a helper fit for him."*

So What Now?

"I will make for him a helper fit for him"?

Remember God's concluding statement from Genesis 1:31 about the totality of creation, including man and woman. *"It was very good."* It (His creation design) is best for us because it comes from an all-wise Creator. It is beautiful. God took delight in what He had done. It is somewhat of a mystery – we may not fully understand all that is encompassed here. But we need to place ourselves under the wise and loving authority of the Almighty God.

God created Adam with a need. His being alone was deficient.

Eve was created by a good, wise, loving God as the answer to his need.

A helper. Fit for him. Equal, but not the same. She was different by God's good design, and her differences would correspond to Adam's need. This design helper element is part of her personhood, much like the physical characteristics that set her apart from her man.

The purpose of this book is to equip and encourage faithful women to pursue lives that reflect their theology, for women to live what they believe. Toward that end, we must determine whether we can give assent to these few basic theological principles before moving ahead.

Sisters, good theology, sound thinking, is to our lives much like our undergarments are to our wardrobe.

Stick with me here. Good underwear goes unseen by the general public (at least it should!) but it provides just the right support and coverage to make the outfit look *fantastic. Without good underwear?* Things sag, and stick, and lump and ... well, you know. A carefully chosen ensemble can be a disaster without the appropriate undergarments. What people see on the outside looks only as good as the stuff underneath.[34]

34 An analogy shared with me by my good friends Karen Hodge and Connie Miller

Good theology? Sound thinking? These are the "support" for our practical lives – what people see on the outside. Our choices, words, decisions are informed by the "undergarment" of our theology! What do we believe about God relative to gender?

God has created all people, men and women, in His image.

God created all people, men and women, equal in His image. Equal does not mean same.

Men and women are different in ways that were designed by God at the time of creation.

And it was *very good.* Are you ready? Let's put this underwear to the test!

Chapter Three

THE FOUR-LETTER WORD

Kathryn Stockett's *The Help* is set in the 1960s in Jackson, Mississippi. Her story is told primarily in the first person by Aibileen Clark and Minny Jackson, African-American maids who clean houses and care for the young children of various white families. As such, they are acquainted with Eugenia "Skeeter," daughter of a prominent white family who employs many African-Americans in the cotton fields, as well as in their home. When she returns home from college, Skeeter begins to see her life and the lives of those around her very differently. As a potential writing project, she asks poignant, thoughtful questions of these women who historically have been incidental characters in the story of her life. As they bravely come to the forefront, "the help" – led by Aibileen and then Minny – reveal a side of Mississippi home life that would change Skeeter (and Stockett's readers) forever.

I read *The Help* in three days. Stockett's story both disturbed and inspired me as I learned for the first time about an era in our collective American history that has been absent from our textbooks. Taking care of, actually *raising* other people's babies, Aibileen would raise *seventeen white children* in her lifetime. It was Aibileen who rocked those babies to sleep. It was Aibileen who taught them to walk. And to talk. Aibileen would potty-train and bathe and spoon-feed other people's babies. She would eventually walk them to school and home again, day after day until each child grew up and went off to school. Then she would begin again, with another family.

In return? Low pay. Long hours. Terrible living conditions. No health care. These women were forced to put their hair up in a rag every day, because the white people assumed "coloreds don't wash their hair."[35] Their employers would count every piece of silver after the polishing was done, to be sure that "the help" hadn't slipped a piece into their perfectly-pressed aprons. Some wealthier white families installed a toilet for their colored help, to protect their own facilities from being soiled.

The help.

With this in our minds, it is no wonder that we vehemently deny the possibility that God might have *designed* women to be "helpers." Our collective conscience recoils, knowing that *no one deserves to be treated that way.* How could such a plan come from the God that we see in Scripture?

Without repeating what has already been clearly put forward in this text: God created **all people, men and women, in His image**. *No one deserves* the kind of treatment that was inflicted on an entire race of people in this country. Having been created in the image of God, all people ought to be held in the highest esteem, valued worthy, and cherished. Regardless of age, gender, race, or socioeconomic status we ought to be, of all creatures, most highly treasured.

These women, the help, whose stories have been told so powerfully by Kathryn Stockett, represent the moral failure of our nation. The superiority and dominance of their white countrymen deserves our collective contempt. We are right in our indignation and we ought to be fiercely committed to protecting people (any people) from the kind of treatment endured by "the help."

35 *The Help*

The Extra Locomotive

While Stockett's portrayal of "the help" is too extreme to serve as our definitive understanding of the word "helper," it is sufficient to give some explanation to our aversion to its application to women in general. Over the years, the term "helper" may have lost some of its dread, but few modern women would welcome the assumptions fundamental to its use.

Merriam-Webster provides this definition for the word "helper": "one that helps; *especially*: a relatively unskilled worker who assists a skilled worker usually by manual labor." Italics theirs. Dictionary.com uses this example to illustrate its definition of "helper": "an extra locomotive attached to a train at the front, middle or rear, especially to provide extra power for climbing a steep grade." Now *that's* inspiring.

The *American Heritage Dictionary* offers the synonym "assistant." Which seems more palatable than "extra locomotive." However, to whatever degree the word "helper" may mean "assistant," we typically assume two things: less-than and for the benefit of someone else. An assistant/helper receives less pay, less respect, and less freedom than her supervisor. Her work is determined by and for the benefit of her boss. In a culture that celebrates self-reliance and self-fulfillment, the very idea of *helping* (which advances the good of someone else) is uninspiring.

Consider this recent advice to working women:

"At work, women are often caught between a rock and a hard place. On the one hand, women like to help. They tend to be more nurturing and better at forming and tending relationships. They tend to help out, pitch in, or do work...when the task is, strictly speaking not their responsibility...however, the practice of mutually empowering [*helping*] in a culture of independence and self-promotion, volunteering to help others achieve is deviant behavior. In fact, taking on the role of 'help' diminishes women in their colleague's eyes."[36]

Today's woman may not bear the weight and shame endured by her African-American sisters of the '60s. Which is welcome progress. However, because we live in a culture increasingly defined by independence and self-promotion, being a "helper" by choice is considered abnormal, unusual or even deviant behavior.

And Yet...

Yet, it's there. Twice in the creation story.

"But for Adam there was not found a helper fit for him."

"I will make for him a helper fit for him."

The word "helper," or "help meet," is the Hebrew word *ezer* and it is used in *every single version/translation* of the Bible in these verses. This word, *ezer*, can be found twenty-one times in the Old Testament. Its New Testament corollary, *parakletos*, is used five times, four times by the Apostle John and once by the writer of Hebrews.

Sisters, this word "helper" is a Biblical word. While I admit that its meaning has been hijacked by the American version of the English language, the fact remains that the use of the word *ezer* by God through Moses, and David, and numerous prophets and then John was not a casual, offhanded choice of language. The Apostle Paul reminds us that *"All Scripture is breathed out by God and profitable..."*[37] All Scripture. Every single word. Breathed out by God. Profitable.

This is not an issue of semantics. Or of poor translation. Or of colloquialisms.

36 www.advancingwomen.com
37 2 Timothy 3:16

All of those potential explanations for God's use of this word in describing His design of woman find themselves lacking when *ezer* is considered in the context of all of Scripture. While pages and pages have been written on the *translation* and *application* of the word *ezer* in this text, my point is simple but sobering: If we are going to be increasingly transformed into the image of Christ this side of heaven, if we are going to *live* what we *believe*, we must live according to the Word. As God intended it. Not as we have culturalized its translation.

It's Not Easy Being Green

I love language. I love words and punctuation and tone. I love the rhythm of words and the cadence of a paragraph. An interesting trend in our language is our assignment of new meaning to old words. Our habit of *redefining* words is intriguing.

My brothers grew up watching Sesame Street. The series that premiered in the fall of 1969 continued its influence on my own children in the early '80s. One of our favorites has always been Kermit the Frog. His angsty, lyrical ballad, "It's not easy being green," was included on the first Sesame Street album that entertained our family when my brothers were little and I can still sing the lyrics today.

"It's not that easy being green. Having to spend each day the color of the leaves ... it seems you blend in with so many other ordinary things."

Kermit's song was about being green. The color. Really, green. He was bemoaning the "blandness" of his skin (is it really skin, on a frog?) and wishing that his were a flashy color, special. Like red or gold.

I looked up the word "green." Webster lists nine definitions for the adjective that are consistent with Kermit's use of the word. These definitions primarily allude to color or shade. Its tenth definition, added sometime in the last decade, reads: "relating to or being an environmentalist political movement; concerned with or supporting environmentalism; tending to preserve environmentalist quality."[38] There is a "Green Party" whose charter lists these six guiding principles: ecological wisdom, social justice, participatory democracy, nonviolence, sustainability, and respect for diversity.[39]

When did "green" *stop* being just a *color*? When did it become the representation of environmentalist policy? Kermit must be glad to know that now it is *popular* and *desirable* to be green. It means you recycle. That you look for products that are "environmentally friendly." It means that now you sort your trash. It takes a lot of work to be green. Kermit was right in the end; it really isn't easy being green.

Lots of words that meant one thing when I was in elementary school have new meanings today.

Fly. It's no longer just a verb. Now it's a compliment. It means "great."

Beef. The infamous commercial for the Wendy's Burger chain that asked, "Where's the beef?" would have new meaning today. Instead of meaning, "where is the meat in your burger" it might mean, "what's your problem"?

Crack. It used to be part of a skipping rhyme. You know, "don't step on the crack or you'll break your mother's back." If only the current meaning of the word were that innocent...

Grill. Not just your average outdoor cooking equipment.

38 www.m-w.com
39 Wikipedia.org/greenparty

Now, to sport a new grill is to have a new set of teeth.

So we're forced to adapt to the new use of these and myriad other words – or we just don't use them at all. Which seems to work. Almost-limitless elasticity is a unique beauty – and curse – of the English language. I'm not sure I've deployed any of the above in the more than 10,000 words that I've written so far in this manuscript.

Ezer, "helper" is not one of those words. We are not in a position to redefine the Word of God. We cannot avoid or replace the language that He has used.

Becoming Eve means recovering our understanding of being an *ezer* from God's heart and mind, not our own.

Defining the *Word* From the Word

Twenty-one times the word *ezer* is used; sixteen times as a self-descriptor by God in the Old Testament. Let's consider just a sampling.

Exodus 18:4 "*for he* [Moses] *said, 'The God of my father was my ezer (help), and delivered me from the sword of Pharaoh.'*"

Deuteronomy 33:26 "*There is none like God, O Jeshurun, who rides through the heavens to your ezer (help)...*"

Psalm 20:1, 2 "*May the Lord answer you in the day of trouble!... May He send you ezer (help) from the sanctuary and give you support from Zion!*"

Psalm 33:20 "*Our soul waits for the Lord; He is our ezer (help) and our shield.*"

Psalm 54:4 "*Behold, God is my ezer (helper); the Lord is the upholder of my life.*"

Psalm 70:5 "*O God, you are my ezer (help) and my deliverer.*"

Do you see a theme here? In each of the above verses, and all but three of the remaining occurrences in the Old Testament, the word *ezer* is used to refer to **God**. God rides to your help. God sends you help. God is our help. God is my help. God. Help.

In the New Testament, John, quoting the Savior, will use the word "helper" four times.

John 14:16 "*And I will ask the Father, and He will give you another* Helper, *to be with you forever,*"

John 14:26 "*the* Helper, *the Holy Spirit, whom the Father will send in my name, he will teach you all things and bring to your remembrance all that I have said to you.*"

John 15:26 "*when the* Helper *comes, whom I will send to you from the Father, the Spirit of truth, who proceeds from the Father, he will bear witness about me.*"

John 16:7 "*Nevertheless, I tell you the truth: it is to your advantage that I go away, for if I do not go away, the* Helper *will not come to you. But if I go, I will send him to you.*"

The word "helper" is used each time in reference to the Holy Spirit. Since God exists in Three Persons, and The Holy Spirit *is* God, we may conclude that these occurrences of the word "Helper" in the New Testament *also* reference God.

What Does It Mean?

We've established the current cultural definition of the word "help." It means passive. Subservient. Inferior. Small.

However, as we thoughtfully consider this word as God uses it to describe *Himself*, the God of the Universe, such descriptors are without merit. The word *ezer* as it is employed in the Bible supplies a picture of God's strength, of His power, of His vitality and wisdom. It informs our theology as it illustrates for us a God who is quick to rescue, to protect, to comfort, and to support.

We think of a helper as one who is weak. But this is God, our helper: *"Who is this King of Glory? The Lord, strong and mighty"* (Psalm 24:8).

We think of a helper as one who is inferior. But this is God, our helper: *"God* reigns *over the nations; God sits on His holy throne"* (Psalm 47:8).

We think of a helper as one who is ignorant and simple. But this is God, our helper: *"O Lord, how manifold are your works! In* wisdom *you have made them all"* (Psalm 104:24).

We think of a helper as one who is timid. But this is God, our helper: *"Contend, O Lord, with those who contend with me; fight against those who fight against me!"* (Psalm 35:1).

This is God. He is our *ezer.*

With few exceptions, this word in Scripture is used primarily for God. And here, in the Genesis account of creation, for Adam's new bride. And for you. *Ezer.*

Are you gaining a vision for becoming Eve?

More Than a Hat

When my children were at home, my friends and I would often discuss the various "hats" that we exchanged throughout a typical day. From the chef hat, to the taxi driver, to search and rescue (that's when we were expected to locate a missing uniform, or homework assignment, or baseball glove), to teacher, to counselor, to nurse. Some were everyday hats. Others we donned just for special occasions. Like police officer on first-solo-drive night. Or wardrobe design (or redesign) on prom night.

My single friends have "hat wardrobes." Emily wears her

teacher hat, her friend hat, her daughter hat, her roommate hat, her leadership team hat, her mentor hat, her counselor hat and her new sister-in-law hat. Candi adds her softball team player hat. Jill adds her home owner/landlord hat.

As we consider what it means to be uniquely feminine, to live with *ezer* – like faith by design, we need to see that *ezer* is more than another hat we wear. It's not another *role* we've been given, or a category for things that we do. John Piper defines living with this perspective of God's design and promises a "disposition." He suggests that it "expresses itself in many different ways depending on the situation… The specific acts that grow out of the disposition vary considerably from relationship to relationship, not to mention culture to culture."[40]

Faith that demonstrates itself in the helper disposition is a feminine expression that applies to every season, every circumstance and every arena of life – every "hat." This is what God had in mind when He fashioned the woman from Adam's rib. That she would be *"for him … a helper."* Remember Grudem's comment: "Genesis 2 does not merely say that Eve *functions* as Adam's helper (one of her many 'hats') in one or two specific events. Rather, it says that God made Eve for the purpose of providing Adam with help, one who *by virtue of creation* would function as Adam's helper."[41]

God made woman for the purpose of providing man with help. Does such a disposition play out differently for a married woman and her husband than for that same woman and her boss? Absolutely. Is it different for single women and their single brothers? Yes. Is there an application for pastors and elders and the women whom they shepherd? Yes. Is there a

40 *What's the Difference?*, Piper, p. 51
41 *Recovering Biblical Manhood and Womanhood*

difference in application between the faith-filled disposition of *helper* in a woman whose husband is walking with the Lord and one who is not? Yes.

But the faith-filled expression of the helper disposition is there. Our goal here is not to define a specific set of behaviors. An attempt to do so would be futile, because it would be limited by whatever circumstances I could enumerate – and that list would be woefully shortsighted. What we must do is discover true femininity that accords with the truth of God's purpose as it was set forth in creation and as it resonates throughout Scripture. We must see that the "helper" design has more to do with attitude, heart, and perspective than about a list of things to do (or not do). It applies whether I am wearing my chef hat, my teacher hat, my director-of-women's-ministry hat, or my wife-of-Chas hat.

Yes, But…

I'm not dismissing men and their unique design as ordained at creation by God. Theirs is a story equally thrilling and full of mystery as ours. The faith-filled disposition of biblical manhood both informs and strengthens our unique disposition to be helpers. However, this book is not written for or to men.

As I've studied to speak and write on this topic, I've been compelled and informed by God's call for biblical manhood. John Piper's definition, expounded on in *What's the Difference?* helps me to know how to pray for my husband, my son, and the men in our church:

"At the heart of mature masculinity is a sense of benevolent responsibility to lead, provide for and protect women in ways appropriate to a man's differing relationships."[42]

42 *What's the Difference?*, p. 23

This solid and compelling description of faith that expresses itself in godly *manhood* gives me a framework for *helper*-inspired thinking. But the danger is that I get distracted by what men are/are not, should or should not be doing. It's so tempting to lament their reluctance to lead, to be discouraged by their lack of sacrifice on our behalf, to despair of their taking godly initiative and then to use all or one of those excuses to explain my own lack of faith and my ungodly feminine disposition.

My faith in the covenant-keeping God does not depend on anyone but Christ. The expression of that faith in my unique helper disposition, designed by God, also depends *solely on Christ.* It is not dependent on whether the men around me are fulfilling their role. This should inspire great hope and passion. As we walk with God, trusting in His presence and promise, we may confidently express our helper design. No matter what our brothers are doing or not doing, around us.

God is doing a work in *me.*

I am a woman.

A daughter of Eve.

A helper.

Where Are We Headed?

It is probably clear by now that this book is not a comprehensive, technical discussion of the issue of gender. That's not my purpose or my personality. There are many texts in Scripture that characterize godly womanhood. If you wanted to construct a holistic, biblical perspective you would need to study *all* of them. Rather, my purpose is to give us a vision for our lives and ministries that is deeply theological, particularly feminine, and kingdom-focused.

These pages should contain enough biblical support to show

why I believe this perspective of gender is in fact *according to the Bible*. I have studied this topic extensively and have read the work of numerous scholars that I trust (and will quote often). It is presented from my understanding of God's covenant love and faithfulness for me. As I've already said, this is *my* journey too – I'm barely past the first few mile markers, with quite a distance to go.

But addressing this difficult issue is not for my benefit alone, nor should it be for yours. What happens here will have dramatic impact on the future of the church and the lives of our neighbors and friends. Gender matters. Individual lives, families, churches, communities, and cultures are at stake. The vision that we have for people is one that ought to compel us to fall on our knees and beg God to change us. It will be *His* work, and it is not only right, but it is good.

Piper has described God's design for manhood and womanhood as a "deeply satisfying fit of grace from a loving God who has the best interests of his creatures at heart."[43] It is, therefore, "fulfilling in the deepest sense of that word."[44] Returning to our theology, we cling to the knowledge that God's plan for us is best. Our becoming Eve brings Him glory . . . it will bring us joy!

Here We Go

With that in mind, here's a simple acrostic that we will use for the remainder of our study of God's design for the *helper* disposition of women. Acrostics can strengthen our memory. On a recent trip to the grocery store, I needed **g**rapes, **a**pples, **p**ears, and **s**trawberries for a fruit salad recipe. Remembering GAPS meant I didn't have to write it down. (Who needs a list?)

43 *What's the Difference?*, p. 16
44 ibid.

Let's consider each of the letters in the word "help." As you read, keep in mind where we began. This information is good and sound and biblical. But it will not be enough. Remember the "trio of hope." Sound theology – good information – is critical. But it must be accompanied with *repentance* and *faith that lives practically.* You must consider the following while asking the Holy Spirit to reveal your own rebellion and to give you repentance and faith. What you know to be true about God and how desperately you cling to Him is the "hinge-pin" of this new perspective.

A Hedge of Protection

The disposition of *helper* as God designed it, particularly in women, demonstrates itself in her desire to create a **h**edge of protection around the people entrusted to her care.

Deuteronomy 33:7 says, *"I will contend for him, and be an ezer against his adversaries,"* and Psalm 33:20 recounts, *"Our soul waits for the Lord for He is our ezer and our shield."* Both of these verses use a literary tool called synthetic parallelism. This allows the author to elaborate on the meaning of a word by using another word to illustrate his intent. In this case, the word *ezer* is further illustrated by the words "contend" and "shield." These verses depict God as our helper when He *rescues* us from our enemies and when He creates a *safe place* for us to rest.

How have you experienced this aspect of the nature of God? As you recall this expression of His work in your life, consider how such a disposition might characterize godly women. What difference would it make for our families, our neighbors, and our churches for God to work in us to be proactive in our care for them? For their comfort and security to be our Christ-like goal? What keeps us from such a disposition?

Create a Culture of Empathy

The God-designed disposition of *helper* also demonstrates itself in a woman's ability to empathize with others – those who are much like her and others who are very different.

The psalmist describes the Lord, *"O Lord, you have azer (helped) me and comforted me"*[45] and again, *"He delivers the needy when he calls, the poor and him who has no ezer."*[46] This word illustrates the action that God has taken on our behalf as He recognizes our plight, the desperation of our sin and failure, and He *enters into our experience*. The writer of Hebrews would say, *"We do not have a high priest who is unable to sympathize with our weaknesses, but one who in every respect has been tempted as we are, yet without sin."*[47] Jesus entered into, empathized with us by leaving the throne of heaven and becoming a man.

How have you experienced this aspect of the nature of God? As you recall this expression of His work in your life, consider how such a disposition might characterize godly women. What difference might it make for our families, our neighbors, and our churches for God to work in us, enabling us to *enter into the experience of others*? What keeps us from doing so?

Lifting and Sustaining

The God-given disposition of a *helper* is one who lifts people out of despair and discouragement and supports them in their struggle.

The Psalmist cried out *"May He send you ezer from the sanctuary and grant you support from Zion"*[48] and, in a more personal

45 Psalm 86:17
46 Psalm 72:12; This variation of the word "help" is the Hebrew word *azar*
47 Hebrews 4:15
48 Psalm 20:2

moment David declares: *"Surely God is my ezer; the Lord is the one who sustains me."*[49] Over and over throughout his life and reign, David's confidence would be shaken, his character and leadership ability in question, his family dynamics a mess. And yet the Lord continually reminded him of *who* he was and *to whom* He belonged. Regularly, God lifted David – out of fear, out of despair, out of discouragement, out of confusion. While not perfect, David is remembered as "*a man after God's own heart.*"[50]

How have you experienced this aspect of the nature of God? As you recall this expression of His work in your life, consider how such a disposition might characterize godly women. What if, as we exercise our faith in *this* God, we were slow, reticent even, to criticize and dismiss in favor of lifting and supporting? What does our rebellion look like?

Promoting the Benefit of Others

The God-given disposition of a *helper* is characterized by the selfless promotion of others to accomplish His plans and purposes.

David's career began in the field. With the sheep. I Samuel 16 recounts the story of Samuel's search, at the Lord's command, for Israel's new king. He went to the house of Jesse, who was the father of numerous successful, handsome, strong sons. Having eliminated Eliab, Abinadab, Shammah, and four others, Samuel wondered which of the sons the Lord would choose, if not these. After Jesse offered David, the youngest, least qualified and prepared, Samuel heard from the Lord, *"Arise, anoint him, for this is he."*[51] Samuel did as the Lord commanded, and the rest

49 Psalm 54:4
50 1 Samuel 13:14, Acts 13:22
51 1 Samuel 16:12

– as they say – is history. Ethan, the Ezrahite, would describe this moment in Psalm 89: *"I [God] have granted ezer to one who is mighty; I have exalted one chosen from the people."* It was the Lord who promoted David. It was the Lord who established him, helping the scrawny little shepherd to reach his full potential.

How have you experienced this aspect of the nature of God? As you recall this expression of His work in your life, consider how such a disposition might characterize godly women. What would it mean for God to work in us to help others to reach their potential, to promote the plans and ideas of others, to encourage their gifts, passions, and abilities so that they advance the kingdom of God? *Why don't we do so?*

A Tall Order

Creating a **H**edge of protection

Cultivating **E**mpathy

Lifting and sustaining

Promoting the benefit of others

Do you see the *disposition* that Piper alluded to? Being created in the *helper* design is not another role, or hat that we wear. It is a posture that we assume by faith, an attitude that we adopt by faith, a disposition that we aspire to because of our faith in the God who created us and sustains us in these ways from one moment to the next. This is *becoming Eve.* Leaning into such a disposition seems like a lot to ask. And, honestly, it is. (Remember the "molehill/mountain" thing?)

As I write today, my own journey wavers. I have struggled to put down just a few hundred words because I am distracted by my own failure. The enemy reminds me of my old ways in my marriage, with my children and in ministry. Which doesn't require a long memory. I have failed *this week*. Well, yesterday, to be candid. I am insecure about my own ability to articulate what I don't faithfully demonstrate personally.

We have, throughout these pages, pressed the importance of theology and faith. But we must also understand that to exercise our trust in the steadfast love of God and live in light of His creation design for us as women is not effortless. There is an important interplay between the work of God in our lives (faith) and our own responsibility to *engage* in that work. This is the tension revealed in Paul's letter to his friends the Philippians: *"Continue to work out your own salvation, for it is God who works in you to will and to work for His good pleasure."*[52] It is God who does the work, but I must *continue*. It's a nuance that I don't have the space to elaborate on (and, admittedly I don't fully understand it!), but before going forward it must be acknowledged.

Living in light of what we believe to be true is not easy, whether it's in the arena of gender, or finances, or relationships, or time management. It is in fact hard, and I am not the "poster child" for such a life.

However, hard is not bad. It's just hard. We have, in our day, equated "hard" with something to avoid. We don't like hard work, hard questions, or hard circumstances. We have made it our life's ambition to steer clear of "hard" at all cost.

But the idea of "life-with-God-is-not-easy" was one of the final topics of conversation between Jesus and His friends before He left them for heaven. After His promise of the Spirit *Ezer's* presence, John records Jesus leaving His disciples with these words: *"in the world you will have tribulation [trouble]."*[53] No

52 Philippians 2:12, 13
53 John 16:33

question about it. Trouble is a guarantee for the life of a Christ-follower. Why are we constantly surprised by the tribulation, the hardship of life this side of heaven? Jesus assured us it would be here.

Alex and Brett Harris list "five kinds of hard" that provide the foundation for their book *Do Hard Things*. I am struck by how their list defines my experience of clinging to my faith. According to the Harris brothers, here's what's hard:

- Things that are outside of your comfort zone.
- Things that go beyond what is expected or required.
- Things that are too big to accomplish alone.
- Things that don't earn an immediate payoff.
- Things that challenge the cultural norm.[54]

Here's how that applies to my becoming Eve:

Living in light of my faith *as a woman* is out of my comfort zone.

No one except God really expects this of me.

On my own I am self-protecting, self-preserving and self-promoting. Left to myself, I will never be anything else. Desperately wicked.

The immediate "payoff" for this kind of walk with God cannot be quantified. The "gain" is often not external, meaning *sometimes nobody notices except me.*

The cultural norm feeds my self-centered womanhood. Even the *discussion* of anything different challenges the cultural norm, making pretty much everybody uncomfortable.

If the Harrises would give me personal license, I would add a sixth point to the list:

- Things that are hard are often lonely.

54 *Do Hard Things*, Alex & Brett Harris

In his devotional *My Utmost for His Highest,* Oswald Chambers says: "If we are going to live as disciples of Jesus, we have to remember that all noble things are difficult. The Christian life is gloriously difficult, but the difficulty does not make us faint and cave in, it rouses us up to overcome."[55] Chambers goes on to suggest that God actually *orchestrates* difficulty in our lives to "test us for all we are worth,"[56] a notion heartily supported by Scriptures such as Deuteronomy 8:2: *"And you will remember the whole way the Lord your God has led you these forty years in the wilderness, that He might humble you, testing you to know what is in your heart."*

So how about we rouse ourselves and cry out to God to increase our faith and give us the capacity to live in light of what we know is true about Him! His design for us, women and men, comes out of His loving kindness to us. He will never leave us, but will always protect, preserve and lift us up. This is His covenant promise. *"I am your God; you are my people."* Even if it's hard, let's discover what it means to live with complete confidence in the Designer, according to His design, as an *ezer.*

Not a companion.

Or a lover.

A partner.

A friend.

But a *helper.* One who is *fit for man.* Suitable and perfectly planned.

Single friends: do not stop reading. *This is for you.*

Childish Things

I have a friend who was a third-grade teacher. While painting

55 *My Utmost for His Highest,* Oswald Chambers
56 ibid.

a craft project with her class, one of her students kept asking if he needed to add a "jacket." It took Judy a few minutes to figure out that he meant *"coat."* He wondered if he could add another "coat" of paint. Smile.

Everyone has stories of mixed up vocabulary from childhood. Paul speaks to such thinking in his letter to the Corinthians. *"When I was a child, I spoke like a child, I thought like a child, I reasoned like a child. When I became a man, I gave up childish ways."*[57]

I realize what's at risk here. I've taught this material to enough audiences to know that to affirm and adopt the biblical view of the word "helper" and to seek to live in faith accordingly is daunting, and perhaps not very appealing (yet). But our *unbiblical thinking* is childish and immature. It is time to put away childish things.

With Chambers, however, this is my hope: "Thank God He does give us difficult things to do! His salvation is a glad thing, but it is also a heroic, holy thing. It tests us for all we are worth. Jesus is bringing many 'sons' unto glory, and God will not shield us from the requirements of a son. God's grace turns out men and women with a strong family likeness to Jesus Christ, not milksops [indecisive, spoiled weaklings]. It takes a tremendous amount of discipline to live the noble life of a disciple of Jesus in actual things. It is always necessary to make an effort to be noble."

Want to be a testimony to the grace of God? To be noble together? It's a tall order, but wouldn't you love to be introduced by the Son to the Father as "my noble woman and *ezer* disciple"?

Let's put away childish things and look forward to the heroic "becoming" that God had in mind from the beginning.

57 1 Corinthians 13:11

Chapter Four

MORE THAN A ROW OF SHRUBBERY

"H" is for "Hedge Protector"

I serve on a staff team whose senior members are almost all men. You might think that would be awkward, even challenging. I suppose in many such situations there is a tricky relational dynamic, but not in this case. I love these people, every one of them. Karen (my only female senior staff partner) is a trusted colleague, and I am so grateful for each of the guys. I have deep respect for them, personally and professionally. I believe that each of the other staff members knows how much I care about them, and I think they know that I am *for them* – for their effective ministry and rich personal lives.

This has not always been the case. Actually, to be clear, it *has* always been the case that I have thoroughly enjoyed the people on our staff team – even as it has morphed over the years. I have considered this a sweet blessing. But several years ago, I was confronted by the reality that my affection was not necessarily reciprocated. I arrived early for a meeting with our then administrative pastor and, since I was early, I made casual conversation with Sarah, his assistant who was a good friend. She made an offhand remark that I expect she meant as humor, but it resonated with me deeply and the Lord has used it powerfully over the years in my life.

"You know, Susan," she said, "when you come over here for a meeting with one of these guys, it is almost as if they are preparing for battle. I wouldn't say they are 'afraid,' but they are definitely on the defensive." Ouch. I was stunned, and sufficiently humbled. I remember thinking about that over the next few days and feeling so sad. The very last thing that I wanted was to bully and intimidate these men who were my spiritual brothers. Sigh.

The faith-filled disposition of a *helper*, designed by God and made in His *ezer* image, demonstrates itself in her desire to cultivate and tend a **H**edge of protection around the people entrusted to her care. This means, at least in part, that people *feel safe* with her. This aspect of her womanhood is informed by the Word and rooted in her faith. Her experience of such safety and security found in the steadfast love of God informs her ability to create a safe place and become a woman who can be trusted. Me? Not so much. I had a lot to learn.

Windshield Wipers and Other Great Lessons about God

I love my car. I'm not really a car-loving kind of person, but I love this car because it is very comfortable and snazzy and it is the *one place* where I know I can be completely by myself. I can control the music, and the temperature (think heated seats! Ahhhhh.....). I almost always have my morning coffee and a few minutes with the Lord in my car. Sitting in the parking lot.

One of the many features that I love about my car is the automated windshield wipers. I love them. When it rains, they come on by themselves (thus the term "automated"). And the speed at which they swipe my windshield adjusts automatically. It is a modern miracle to me that when it's just drizzling they are intermittent, but when it is pouring they pick up speed, clearing the windshield efficiently so I can drive safely.

What if my snazzy car came without a windshield? A heavy rain, even a drizzle, would definitely dampen my travel. But driving windshield-less, rain might be the least of my worries. A particularly strong wind or, worse, a wayward rock would pose a serious threat if my windshield were missing. How much thought have you given to the protection offered by that piece of glass – the windshield?

It is an analogy that has its limits, but our generation is a bit lacking in its appreciation for the value of a shield. Not so the Hebrew people.

Genesis 15:1 is a familiar passage that records God's covenant with Abram, but it begins with these words: "*After these things* [the rescue of Lot and the blessing of Melchizedek] *the word of the Lord came to Abram in a vision: 'Fear not, Abram, I am your shield; your reward shall be very great.'*" The root word in the original language for "shield" in this text means, "hedge around something or someone for protection." Here, the Lord says to Abram, "I am the hedge around you to protect you." How grateful am I for those words in the face of my greatest fear?

God is called our "shield" over fifteen times in the Psalms. Psalm 33:20 connects that illustration to the image of God as *ezer. "Our soul waits for the Lord for He is our* ezer *and our shield."* The shield was a well-known part of ancient armor; such a metaphor would not have been lost on its earliest reader. At a time in history when swords and spears and arrows were the offensive weapons of the day, the shield for defense was typically made of tough and thick hides, fastened to a rim. The rim attached to the left arm of the warrior so that, when attacked, the shield could be thrown before the body, protecting him from mortal danger.

Three times in Psalm 115:9-11, the Psalmist reminds the people of God their *helper* and their shield: *"O Israel, trust in the Lord! He is their ezer and their shield. O House of Aaron, trust in the Lord! He is their ezer and their shield. You who fear the Lord, trust in the Lord! He is their ezer and their shield."* It is no wonder that Charles Spurgeon, in his great *Treasury of David*, writes: "Our soul, our life, must hang upon God; we are not to trust Him with a few gewgaws [19th-century bling or baubles] but with all we have and are."[58]

The Contender

In Deuteronomy 33, we find another occasion of God's image as One who *helps*. As Moses faces his death, he blesses each of the twelve tribes of the people of Israel. Benjamin would be "*surrounded by the High God.*" Joseph would be blessed with "*the choicest gifts of heaven above.*" Zebulon, "*the abundance of the seas and the hidden treasures of the sand.*" Naphtali would be *"sated with favor."*

To Judah he says: *"I* [God] *will contend for him and be a help* [ezer] *against his adversaries."* At first glance, this blessing may seem a little lackluster, but remember the significance of *this tribe*. From the tribe of Judah would come King David. And from David? Matthew 1:17: "*So all the generations from Abraham to David were fourteen generations, and from David to the deportation to Babylon fourteen generations, and from the deportation to Babylon to the Christ fourteen generations.*"

Twenty eight generations would pass between David and Jesus, but in all that time, David's tribe of Judah – the smallest of the nations – survived despite repeated threats from the Ammonites, Philistines, Moabites, Edomites, Assyrians, Egyptians and Babylonians. In his commentary on this verse, John Wesley explains: "Thou wilt preserve this tribe in a special manner, so that his enemies shall not be able to ruin it, as they will do other

58 *Treasury of David*, Psalm 115:9-11

tribes, and that for the sake of the Messiah who shall spring out of it."[59]

How would little Judah survive? God. The Helper and Contender.

The Thread of Helper-Protector Theology

This theology of God our Helper who is our shield and contender resonates throughout all of Scripture. The Old Testament narrative of the history of the people of God includes one account after another of God's *helper* image as He again and again provides protection of His chosen nation. From their dramatic escape from the fierce army of the Egyptians to the intimate and personal care of the widow Naomi and her daughter-in-law Ruth; from Esther in the court of the crazy king Xerxes to the demise of the Assyrian army by a mysterious disease, God's *helper* image as a shield and contender is vividly clear.

New Testament theology continues this theme. Perhaps the most concise account of God's relentless protection of His children is found indirectly in Paul's second letter to the Corinthians. Here the great theologian listed the perils that he had already faced in his life and ministry. Consider how Paul experienced Psalm 33:20 and Deuteronomy 33:7: "*Five times I received at the hands of the Jews the forty lashes less one. Three times I was beaten with rods. Once I was stoned. Three times I was shipwrecked; a night and a day I was adrift at sea; on frequent journeys, in danger from rivers, danger from robbers, danger from my own people, danger from Gentiles, danger in the city, danger in the wilderness, danger at sea, danger from false brothers; in toil and hardship, through many a sleepless night, in hunger and thirst, often without*

59 *John Wesley's Explanatory Notes,* Deuteronomy 33:7

food, in cold and exposure."[60] Such a story, were it produced by Hollywood today, would appear ridiculously melodramatic. How is it possible that Paul survived such a litany of danger? *"Our soul waits for the Lord, for He is our ezer and our shield."* God the helper-shield, the helper-contender. This was Paul's living reality.

The hymn writer who penned "O God Our Help in Ages Past" captured this thread of redemptive theology for our generation:

"Under the shadow of Thy throne,

Thy saints have dwelt secure.

Sufficient is Thine arm alone

And our defense is sure."

That said, I suspect some of you are pondering: If God is truly our *helper-protector*, why did He *not* protect me from ________________ (fill in the blank with your own heartache).

That is a much deeper and more sober subject than I can give proper attention in this text. It is true that sometimes God does not *appear* to protect and preserve His people. Sometimes it *seems like* He is not paying attention at all.

I have had these moments … many of them … in my own life with God. I do not want to offer trite and simple answers. What I *do* know is that the words recorded for us in the Scriptures are *true*, *timeless*, and *pervasive*. They apply to all of life and to every situation. And sometimes that's all we have. We, along with all of the saints for thousands of years before us, must believe in the character of God as revealed in His Word and the economy of eternity – regardless of what *appears* to be true.

Perhaps this next section will give perspective to this nuance

60 2 Corinthians 11:24-28

of God's very real and true helper image. He is the shield and contender in *every* circumstance for His weary and disheartened children. Be encouraged.

Christ Alone

We may not leave this discussion of our *helper* God, the shield and contender, without acknowledging the ultimate fulfillment in the person of Christ. As the Israelites were protected and preserved, as the tribe of Judah triumphed for more than twenty eight generations, as Naomi and Ruth and Esther experienced the nature of God their shield and contender, so God's elect today are blessed and protected in Christ. As Paul's life was redeemed, saved from certain death time and again, so we are rescued and redeemed in the person and work of the Savior. By His blood, He brought down the wall that separated God and man, thus protecting and preserving His people for all generations. Christ is our ultimate Shield and Contender.

Our bodies are eventually going to wither and die. In fact, all but one of the disciples were killed because of their kinship to the Savior. However, their souls and ours will live forever. Nancy Guthrie writes: "God knows that you and I need protection from judgment, which is going to fall, flowing out of divine justice. So he sent us a Protector in the form of a vulnerable baby, a Savior who is no less than his own Son. 'For God did not send his Son into the world to condemn the world, but to save the world through him'[61]. As we hide ourselves in the person and work of Jesus, we find shelter from the sure and certain judgment of the last day."[62] The ultimate protection from eternal death was secured by the provision of the Son's sacrifice on our behalf.

61 John 3:17
62 "Can I really expect God to protect me?" *Christianity Today,* October 2005

It is with such confidence that we claim, together with the Apostle Paul: "*Therefore, since we have been justified by faith, we have peace with God through our Lord Jesus Christ. Through him we have also obtained access by faith into this grace in which we stand, and we rejoice in hope of the glory of God.*"[63]

This, sisters, is the theology that informs our *becoming Eve*. It is this understanding of WHO GOD IS that is the underpinning foundation for how we will live. It is both our *knowledge* of God, our *ezer*-shield and contender, and our experience of His protection and provision that informs and inflames our desire to become His *ezer* image-bearers.

What Does All of This Have to Do With a Hedge?

Remember that the first instance of the word "shield," found in Genesis 15:1, encompassed the idea of a "hedge around something or someone for protection." It is this word-picture that will give us the first of four aspects of our image-bearing as *helpers*: the hedge of protection.

It's a phrase that I have heard all of my life. I'm not exactly sure when it became a viable phrase in Christian-ese, but I can remember my mother praying for a *hedge of protection* around my father when he traveled. Our pastor prays for a *hedge of protection* around missionaries. I've prayed for the hedge myself, around my children, my husband, my siblings, and various and sundry people who needed to be hedged.

But where did the phrase come from? Christian comedian Tim Hawkins asks: "A hedge, huh? I don't mean to complain, [but] is that the best you can do? How about a thick cement wall – with some razor wire!"[64] He goes on to wonder at our

63 Romans 5:1, 2
64 "Hedge of Protection," Tim Hawkins, YouTube®

habit of "praying for shrubbery," suggesting that perhaps our prayers are more rote than informed and wondering if that's the best we can do.

While Hawkins' humor is refreshing, it is not exactly accurate to imply that the hedge-of-protection prayer is trite or unbiblical. It is, in fact, neither. It is true that the exact phrase does not occur anywhere in Scripture; however, the concept is evident in various biblical accounts.

It is likely that the phrase originates from the discourse between God and Satan that takes place at the very beginning of the story of Job. Having noted the wealth and prosperity of Job, the Lord God described him to Satan as a *"blameless and upright man, who fears God and turns away from evil."*[65] Satan's scornful response suggested that Job was not as righteous as he seemed: *"Does Job fear God for no reason? Have you not put a* hedge around him *and his house and all that he has, on every side? You have blessed the work of his hands, and his possessions have increased in the land."*[66] Satan's indictment suggested that Job's godliness was not genuine but rather a result of God's having "hedged him in" to protect his family and allow them to prosper without interference.

In this case, the "hedge" referred to by Satan was a clear boundary. It defined ownership and restricted Satan's access: Job and his family belonged to God. Only God had the prerogative to determine if and when to allow evil and heartache to invade the lives of His people.[67]

65 Job 1:8

66 Job 1:9, 10

67 When God removed the hedge of protection, Job and his family suffered unimaginable trauma. But God never stopped protecting Job. This is one of those circumstances in which we see God allowing Job's suffering with the ultimate goal of his eternal security. Job's life with God is an example of God's unrelenting interest in the protection of our souls, even at the cost of our comfort. A story for another book, but worth noting.

In some of the finer neighborhoods in our city, large homes sit well off the road, surrounded by lush, well-manicured lawns and beautifully landscaped flower beds. Often, the property is set apart from the street and the neighbors by a neatly trimmed, distinct green hedge. The hedge serves as a border, much like a city wall or a tall fence.

The idea of a protective boundary in the form of a hedge is not unique to Job's story. Again and again throughout the Old Testament, the hedge word-picture is employed to describe the idea of security, boundary, and protection.[68] This idea of a *helper hedge* is more than a row of lovely shrubbery. It is, instead, a clear and consistent picture of the nature of God as He helps His people by protecting and preserving them. God was a hedge for Abram, and Joseph and Jacob and Moses. God was a hedge for Peter, and Paul and Timothy and James.

So how does that inform my *disposition* as a *helper*?

Where the Wild Things Are

As we faithfully consider the *helper* nature of God revealed in the pages of Scripture, we see His people threatened by Satan, by mortal enemies, by illness, by famine, by nature, and by the power of evil kings. Each of those threats is no less real for the people of God today. So what is a godly woman to do? Knowing that God alone is the ultimate Hedge of Protection, what does it look like to bear this *helper* image of God as a part of His original plan?

My sister and I each had a room on the third floor of our home when we were in middle school. I have great memories of listening to record albums, singing along with Karen Carpenter into my hairbrush microphone while Leslie sang back up. Leslie

68 See Isaiah 5:5, Jeremiah 49:3, Hosea 2:6,7

and I were such good friends and we spent many nights sleeping not in our own rooms, but together in one or the other's room.

On one such evening, we were lying in bed quietly talking and laughing. At some point, one of us noticed a black slithery looking thing at the end of the bed. Suddenly, our laughter became frantically whispered theories about what the slithery-looking-thing *was* and how it got there.

As he always did, Dad came to our rescue, saving us from certain death (or at least maiming) by the slithery-looking thing, aka *navy blue panty hose* that *someone* had failed to put in the hamper. (I'm dating myself; girls, remember the blue panty hose days?) It's amazing how threatening ordinary things appear in the darkness.

The risk of navy blue panty hose notwithstanding, what are the *real* dangers that threaten us?

Well, there are the obvious things. Like natural disasters. This year alone, we have read in our newspapers about flooding, deadly tornadoes, raging fires, and storms that have wreaked havoc on entire communities. Even when the damage is "mild," like the results of the recent rainy season that we have had in my state, local businesses are impacted, forcing delays in production, loss of revenue and decreased wages.

Violence invades the lives of people in our neighborhoods more often than we'd like to think. For the first six months of this year, these statistics represent crime in my city:[69]

19 homicides
699 robberies
115 rapes
1161 aggravated assaults
653 vehicle thefts
93 arson cases

69 http://charmeck.org/city/charlotte/CMPD/safety/CrimeStat/Pages/default.aspx

Daily stories from our local paper include headlines like "Man faces charges after fatal wreck," "Shots fired into house, killing two," and "Drive by shooting remains unsolved." Other accounts include everything from fraud to a machete attack. And I would have thought this is a fairly safe city.

The economy is dicey. Healthcare is complicated. Jobs are hard to find.

These are just a few of the *tangible* fears that threaten to shipwreck our lives or the lives of those that we love. What about the not-so-tangible challenges that strike fear in the hearts of even brave men (and women)? Like failure.

One of my single friends teaches high school. She loves her job, but she spends much of her energy trying to manage the panic that lies just beneath the surface – threatening to overwhelm her if she is not the *best* teacher in her department, with the best test scores, the highest ranking of her students, the most commendations by her principal. Her fear of "failure" keeps her captive.

Young mothers are worried about their *children's* failure, so they do everything they can to set the children up for success. Under the guise of providing lots of opportunities, parents schlep children from one activity to the next, hoping that they will excel in some particular area – thus guaranteeing Junior a "leg up" on his future. "Average" is no longer acceptable for many of America's youngest generation.

Tension in our homes, and workplaces, and stadiums, and churches has resulted in as yet unmatched levels of stress for otherwise healthy adults and children. The American Psychological Association reports that 77% of Americans regularly experience physical symptoms caused by stress. Almost 50% of those responding feel their stress level has increased in the past five years. Physical symptoms caused by stress include fatigue, headache, upset stomach, muscle tension, and dizziness.[70] (The only upside to all this stress is the boon in sales for the pharmaceutical industry.)

I sat in the car with my good friend. We had been to see a movie and were chatting afterward. Her husband is facing a serious health crisis. "How can I pray for you," I asked her. She dissolved into tears as she admitted that she was afraid and so sad. She was not ready to lose him, and she had to face that very real possibility. I did not know what to say. What could I offer that would be helpful and not trite? So I did not say much. I held her hand and we simply prayed and cried.

Disappointment and disillusionment characterize much of our experience as reality clashes with hopes and dreams and expectations and things don't turn out as we had planned. Marriages falter and often fail. Careers derail. Children wander. All the "stuff" that we have acquired amounts to nothing more than a tally on an insurance policy.

Fear of failure (our own or the failure of those that we love).

Stress.

Disappointment.

Like the "wild things" in Maurice Sendak's children's fantasy, "They roar their terrible roars, and gnash their terrible teeth, and roll their terrible eyes, and show their terrible claws." But unlike Max, the very small hero in Sendak's story, we are unable to pull off the "magic trick of staring into all their yellow eyes without blinking just once," thus taming our greatest fears.

What's an *ezer* to do?

70 www.statisticbrain.com

A Faith-filled Disposition

Our uniquely feminine disposition flows out of our faith. The Heidelberg Catechism captures what we must know and experience about God as we consider the things that threaten us.

Heidelberg Catechism Question #1: What is your only comfort in life and in death?

Answer: That I am not my own, but belong – body and soul – in life and in death – to my faithful Savior, Jesus Christ. He has fully paid for all my sins with His precious blood, and has set me free from the tyranny of the devil. He also watches over me in such a way that not a hair can fall from my head without the will of my Father in heaven; in fact, all things must work together for my salvation.

That is a mouthful and it is worth our commitment to memory. The authors have captured what I took several thousand words to communicate in the early pages of this chapter. Becoming Eve, a woman who bears the *ezer* image of God as one who cultivates a hedge of protection around the people in her care begins with our experiencing this aspect of His nature ourselves. Informed by texts like Psalm 33:20 and Deuteronomy 33:7 and Psalm 115:9-11, we grow in our faith which overflows into a disposition to be women who proactively seek to preserve and protect the people that God has entrusted to us.

Just what does that *look* like? As we consider the threats that present themselves in our lives, it is clear that we are unable to really *do* anything about them. Unlike the superheroes of our imagination, we cannot turn the path of a tornado or stop the avalanche of rain. We are powerless against the violence that tragically impacts the lives of the people in our neighborhoods and cities. Our efforts to soften the blow of economic disaster make only a paltry dent in the crisis brought on by job loss, serious illness, and costly investments.

But we do have something unique and significant to offer. As God is our shield and contender, as He carefully tends the hedge of protection around us, we reflect His image by proactively caring for our families, our friends, our coworkers, neighbors, and church family. Their comfort and security becomes our faith-filled goal.

A Safe Place

When my brother David was just five years old, my dad and mom adopted him into our family. He came to us from a drug-addicted mother and a father who was in prison. He had many emotional and physical challenges. I remember vividly the way that he used to guard his plate at the dinner table. With one hand, he would shovel his food into his mouth. With the other, he would shield his plate, making sure that no one either ate his food or took the plate away. It took weeks for David to begin to feel safe at our dinner table.

This is the kind of safe place that an *ezer*, by virtue of her faith, establishes. Her home, her office, her classroom, her Bible study group is a place where people instinctively feel the freedom to sigh deeply and make themselves comfortable. The effect has little to do with décor (although a cozy chair and a roaring fireplace go a long way!) and more to do with atmosphere and, well, spirit.

You know what this is like. It is the difference between walking into a classy clothing store where you are greeted formally but with a distinctly condescending chill, and walking into a not-quite-as-classy store whose door is propped open to welcome the fresh air *and* the customer.

It's not so much about cleverly arranged furniture. It's about creating a space that makes people feel welcome, comfortable, and safe. Safe from noise. And chaos. And confusion. Safe to relax. Safe to be honest and vulnerable. To laugh hysterically, or weep uncontrollably. Safe to be beautifully put together, or totally a wreck.

Have you seen those yellow diamond-shaped signs that announce a location as a "safe place"? They are the symbol of an organization called "National Safe Place" whose goal is to provide security, support and guidance for teens who have no place else to turn.[71] Homes and businesses that display the yellow sign are inviting those children and teenagers to find shelter with them.

I wanted our home to be this kind of place when my children were teenagers. Hannah was a cheerleader, so we often had lots of girls and football players in the house. Milas played in a band. A "screamer" band. So his friends came with guitars, and amps, and drums. I tried hard to create a space that was welcoming, and warm and safe. I wanted our home to be a place where they felt comfortable and at ease.

More recently, I've had the great privilege to care for a small group of young professional single women. They come to my house every Tuesday evening for Bible study, and every week I try to have a home-cooked meal prepared for their arrival. Most of these women are working very long days and many do not have the margins to cook for themselves. Serving a simple dinner for them is not necessary, and they certainly don't expect it. But sitting around a table together, enjoying a good meal and just chatting about their lives sets a tone that changes the way that we dig into the Scripture together.

Jesus knew the value of *place*. Mark's Gospel describes a very

71 www.nationalsafeplace.org

busy day of ministry in the life of Jesus and His disciples. Chapter 6:31 records Jesus' invitation to pull back, to find a comfortable place so that they could rest together. *"Come away by yourselves to a desolate place and rest awhile.' For many were coming and going and they had no leisure, even to eat."* There's something about food.

"The ache for home lives in all of us. The safe place where we can go as we are and not be questioned."[72] Jesus' disciples needed that kind of place. Cheerleaders, football players, rockers, and single women all need that kind of place. It's that kind of home, and classroom, and office, and neighborhood that an *ezer* woman of God longs for. By faith, she carefully tends her place(s) as a hedge of protection around the people in her world. Can she change their circumstances? Most often not. But she can create a place where people feel safe and secure and loved – by her Heavenly Father and by His *ezer* image bearer.

A Safe Person

Cultivating a hedge of protection is not just about place. More often, it's about personhood. Going back to movie night with my friend, my car was not the most inviting or comfortable place. In that moment, "place" was less important than just my presence, my attention, and my interest. All I had to do was ask one question and this sweet friend, knowing she was safe with me, was able to cry for the first time since her husband's illness reached this critical state.

One of my all-time favorite story lines from the life of Christ is His relationship to Martha, Mary's oh-so-brassy sister. Theirs is a story for another book, but one of the most intriguing details of Jesus' first recorded interaction with Martha is His

72 *All God's Children Need Traveling Shoes,* Maya Angelou

response to her impertinent and demanding outburst famously recorded in Luke 10.

Jesus was a guest in their home, and Mary sat quietly listening to Jesus teach while Martha slaved away in the kitchen preparing the meal for their guests. Finally, Martha had enough. She likely stomped out of the kitchen, interrupted Jesus' lesson and demanded: "*Lord, do you not care that my sister has left me to serve alone? Tell her then to help me.*" I feel such empathy with this woman. What's significant is not only what Jesus said, but also what He *did not say*. Notice that Jesus did not say: "How dare you speak to me that way!" or, even better, "Martha, why can't you be more like sweet Mary? Look at her. Sitting here listening quietly. You should take a lesson from your sister." What He said were words of tender compassion to a woman who was worn out.

Martha was safe with Jesus. Safe to be frustrated. Safe to be angry, and weary, and disappointed. I'm not suggesting that her approach was necessarily appropriate, but it is worth noting that Jesus did not reprimand her for her attitude. He was more concerned about her soul.

Becoming a woman of God who reflects Him as a protector and preserver means that people have the freedom to be on a journey, to be something less than perfect. They know that they are safe. Safe to be sad. Safe to be discouraged, or worn out, or resentful. Safe to fail. Safe to struggle with doctrine and faith. Safe to disagree.

Which does not mean that we leave them there. Jesus allowed Martha to vent, and then He gently set her straight. He spoke to her with eternity in mind and His kind and thoughtful reprimand had an impact on Martha that changed her life. We'll come back to this important aspect of *ezer* image bearing as we further develop our HELP acrostic, but for now it is enough to note that safety does not mean stagnant.

A helper who tends a hedge of protection in the name of Christ approaches relationships with humility. She acknowledges her own failure and sin, and the grace of God in her life is on display. Having received His grace, she freely offers that grace to others.

The Apostle Paul's life and ministry resound with this humility and grace. He refers to himself as the "*least of the Apostles*"[73] because of his former persecution of the church, and his claim on the incredible grace of God weaves its way throughout his letters. It is no wonder that this man had such an impact on the lives of others. Having received grace, he readily and passionately offered such grace to others, not surprised by their weakness or disappointed by their failure.

Another defining characteristic of this *ezer* disposition is the ability to be present, to be in the moment with people. This is a struggle for those of us who would describe ourselves as "Type A" personalities. I am almost always thinking several hours, if not several days ahead of myself. I used to think that was efficient. Now I realize that it is actually obsessive and, for the person sitting in front of me sharing her heartache, it's just rude. It is not easy to be fully present, to focus and concentrate on the "here and now" in this culture. We are busy. We are distracted. We are typically spinning *many* plates at one time.

How grateful am I that God is not like that. God, who is uniquely *omnipresent,* is fully present in every moment with me. Fully present. I am safe with Him because He is never *not listening*. No matter where I am or who I am with or what I am doing, He is always there. Tending the hedge. Shielding and contending for me. How I want to be like that with people!

73 1 Corinthians 15:9

Not for the Faint of Heart

I hope these few paragraphs have sparked a new way of thinking about what it means to be a woman who is a shield and contender, one whose faith leads her to fulfill her creation-design by cultivating safety – in her environment and personhood. We'll build on this foundation and, in subsequent chapters, we will consider particular ways in which this hedge protecting mindset applies.

This new thinking does not come naturally for most of us. As I think about that scene back in Sarah's office, I wince at my propensity to be demanding and purposefully intimidating. I like to have the upper hand. I am impatient. I interrupt people. I am always in a hurry. In those days, I feel sure that people would not have characterized me as "safe."

Thank you, Sarah.

The crux of Sarah's gracious (if unwitting) admonishment was that those men with whom I labored did not feel safe with me. Instead of reflecting the image of God as a shield and contender, a helper suitable for these brothers, I had (at least in their opinion and to varying degrees) contended *against* them. I have never forgotten that.

This *ezer* transformation has been slow. It is directly informed and influenced by my walk with God, which has not always been consistent. However, my faith in God's protection of me, of the hedge of protection that He has tended, has grown. When I know that He is for me, that He is my shield and contender, I have the confidence to think less about myself and more about the benefit of those around me.

But even on good days, when I am able to see growth in my own life, I am also aware of the cost. Bearing the image of God as a shield and contender puts me at risk, at least in my earth-bound perspective. Tending my place as a hedge of protection means that I must *desire* to make other people comfortable. Which means I might be *uncomfortable.* I must be honest about my own fears and failures, which means I might be judged. Or misunderstood. I must listen more, talk less. Which means I might be dismissed. (Wise words from my mother: "Just because you have an opinion does not mean everyone needs to hear it." I still haven't fully embraced that line of thinking.)

This *ezer*-tender-of-hedges is just not me. But it *is* Christ in me. The display of God's redemptive grace in my life has paved the way for meaningful relationships and ministry. Over the years, as God has kindly revealed to me my own desperate need for Someone to contend for me, I have been taken captive by the Shepherd who *is* my Hedge of protection. The safest place in the world for me is under the shadow of His wing, in the security of His flock, at the foot of the Cross. It is *His* help that has saved me.

What is my only comfort in life and in death? That I am not my own, but belong – body and soul – in life and in death – to my faithful Savior, Jesus Christ. This is the theology of the "H" in my helper disposition. This is *my* hedge, and it is the doctrine that both informs and inflames my passion to *become Eve*, a woman who is a helper-shield and contender.

What difference would it make for women to be changed by their own experience of the comfort of God in Christ? What difference for our families, our neighbors, and our churches for God to work in us to be proactive in our care for them? For their comfort and security to be our Christ-like goal? Hang on to your navy blue panty hose. We'll come back to this!

Chapter Five

PUT YOUR FINGER HERE

"E" is for "Empathizer"

I recently came across a website that offered an interactive experience of what it was like to be in Haiti during and after the 7.0 earthquake that hit that country in 2010. Visitors to the website may see the experience through the eyes of a journalist, a survivor or an aid worker. I worked my way through all three. By the end, I was near tears and physically exhausted.

But something else happened as I sat in the comfort of my own study, clicking away on my mouse with one hand and sipping my tall-decaf-sugar-free-vanilla-breve-extra foam latte in the other. To whatever degree is possible on this side of the continent, I felt the pain of those people. My stomach knotted, my head pounded and my heart ached, with the despair, defeat, and grief of an entire country.

Harper Lee, in her classic *To Kill a Mockingbird*, records this simply-loaded comment from father to daughter: "You never really understand a person until you consider things from his point of view, ... until you climb into his skin and walk around in it." It has been years since I read this text, but the sentiment resonates with my experience. I did not *actually* put on that beautiful black Haitian skin and walk around, barefoot, and practically naked except for blood-soaked bandages. I did not find my place among the thousands in the refugee camp. I have not walked the streets of burned-out buildings, dangerously crumbling by bits and pieces. I did not hold my own baby while she died in my arms. But I came about as close as I can.

And it has changed me.

We have seen that the faith-filled disposition of a *helper*, designed by God and made in His own *ezer* image, demonstrates itself in her desire to cultivate and tend a **H**edge of protection. A second characteristic of this uniquely feminine disposition is the growing capacity to **E**mpathize with others, to "climb into their skin and walk around in it." This aspect of "*ezerhood*" is informed by Scripture and rooted in faith. It is the God-given ability to redemptively *remember*, and the desire to understand what we have not experienced.

"I Feel Your Pain"

It was during his first presidential campaign in the spring of 1992 that Bill Clinton immortalized the phrase, "I feel your pain." He was responding to Bob Rafsky, an AIDS activist at a New York City fundraiser who challenged him to take a stand and address the AIDS epidemic in America. That phrase, immortalized on *Saturday Night Live*, has become one of our generation's best-known clichés.

Whether or not Mr. Clinton did in fact feel the pain of Mr. Rafsky, his comment introduced a relatively new platform for politicians: empathy. A candidate's ability to empathize with the people – to feel their pain – has become a central political issue on the landscape of pundits and pollsters in America.

Psychology Today suggests that empathy is "the experience of understanding another person's condition from their perspective."[74] *Merriam Webster* goes a bit further: "the action of understanding, being aware of, being sensitive to and vicariously experiencing the feelings, thoughts and experiences of

74 www.psychologytoday.com/basics/empathy

another."[75] The original language suggests the capacity to "feel into" or "suffer into" the experience of another.

The Far-reaching Empathy of God

King David was a man who understood pain. His life and reign, preserved in the pages of 1 & 2 Samuel, 1 & 2 Kings and 1 & 2 Chronicles, was marked by danger, treachery, deceit, treason, and devastating loss. He spent much of his adult life either in pursuit of his enemies or in hiding from them. His own sin would have ramifications for his family for generations.

And yet, the Scripture refers to David as "a man after God's own heart."[76] The psalms reflect so much of David's walk with God that they are, for us, a window into his soul and a mirror for our own. Psalm 86 is one of those windows. It is titled simply "A Prayer of David" and it is one of only five psalms so titled. The psalm begins with David's request of the Lord: "*Incline your ear, O LORD, and answer me ... preserve my life ... be gracious to me ... gladden the soul of your servant ... give ear ... listen to my plea ...* " Then, having made his request, David shifts gears and preaches to himself about the character and nature of God. He reminds himself of God's greatness, His glory, His steadfast love, His deliverance, His mercy, His grace, His patience, His faithfulness, His strength. These verses are a *litany* (or list) of praises that would soothe David's worn-out soul and set his heart and mind on a foundation of truth. These are his closing words: "*Show me a sign of your favor, that those who hate me may see and be put to shame because you, LORD, have helped [ezer] me and* comforted *me.*"

While the word "empathy" is not specifically used in Scripture, the Hebrew words translated "comfort" (*chanan* and

75 www.merriam-webster.com
76 1 Samuel 13:13, 14

nacham) are defined as "comfort; ease; being moved to pity; to console; to have compassion." It is the word *nacham* that David deploys in Psalm 86:17, describing the nature of God as his *ezer.* Both words echo our understanding of "empathy" and together they occur more than 125 times in the Old Testament – 42 times in the psalms alone.

David recognized God as His *ezer.* God would *help* David and *comfort* him. He would "feel into" David's suffering. His fear. His anxiety. His heartache. His disappointment. He empathized with David, actually feeling his pain. Charles Spurgeon comments: "Those whom He helps, he also consoles."[77] Augustine would agree, "He hast helped me in struggle and comforted me in sorrow." I suspect that even as he penned the rich, theocentric words of Psalm 86, David experienced the empathy and comfort of His Lord.

The Thread of Helper-Empathizer Theology

This theology of God our Helper who empathizes with us, comforts, and consoles us, resonates throughout all of Scripture. The Psalmist is most prolific here:

"*Thou art with me. Thy rod and thy staff, they comfort me.*"[78]

"*You will increase my greatness and comfort me again.*"[79]

"*Let your steadfast love comfort me.*"[80]

The idea of a God who does not stand far off, removed and distant from our agony, was one that captivated the heart of David. He sometimes seems to hang on to this truth with desperate confidence, the empathy and comfort of the Most High God

77 Charles Spurgeon, exposition of Psalm 86
78 Psalm 23:4
79 Psalm 71:21
80 Psalm 119:76

being his lifeline to faith and hope.

The prophet Isaiah would do the same for the people of Israel. Isaiah 40:1 captures his plea, *"Comfort, comfort my people, says your God."* And again in 49:13: *"The Lord has comforted his people and will have compassion on his afflicted."* We know in hindsight what the prophet knew only dimly: that Jesus would be the ultimate Comforter. That it would be through Jesus that God would demonstrate the ultimate act of empathy. Jesus would physically *enter into our pain*, delivering comfort that would lead to abundant life on earth and ultimately eternity in heaven.

John 14 records the tender empathy of Christ as He anticipates the challenges that His friends would experience in the days, months, years, and generations after His return to heaven. *"I will ask the Father,"* He says in verse 16, *"and He will give you another Helper."* The Greek word used here is *parakletos*; it means "comforter." This is the first of four occasions that Jesus would refer to the Comforter's coming for the benefit of the church. This Comforter would "remind" the people of what they had heard from the Savior. He would be with them and help them and bring them hope.

Samuel Martin, in his book *The Biblical Illustrator* has said: "To what shall we liken comfort? It is like copious and heavy dew to withering flowers. It is like rain to the parched and thirsty earth. It is like the sight of coast and harbor to the mariner, when the sea is rough and the sky is stormy."[81] Dew to withering flowers. Rain to the parched earth. The sight of coast and harbor. This has been the nature of God long before the beginning of time. It is His nature as it is given to us in the person of Christ. And it is His nature that we experience in the person and presence of the Holy Spirit. *Nacham.*

81 www.sermonpreps.com

Put Your Finger Here

The nature of God in Christ as *ezer*-empathizer resonates throughout Jesus' years on earth. Matthew, in his description of Jesus' feelings for the people of Israel, says: "*He had compassion for them, because they were harassed and helpless.*"[82] The New Living Translation puts it this way: "*He felt great pity for the crowds that came, because their problems were so great and they didn't know where to go for help.*" Divine empathy. Jesus suffers with the crowd. He is not separated from their struggle, but shares their experience.

One of the most poignant illustrations of this aspect of the nature of Christ is seen eight days after His resurrection. You might remember that Jesus appeared to His disciples on the evening of resurrection day in the upper room.

Sadly, Thomas missed it. For some reason, he was not with his friends when Jesus arrived in the room. So the other disciples found him (I love that they didn't just kick him out of their club) and told him about Jesus' appearing. Thomas' response became his legacy.

"*Unless I see in his hands the mark of nails, and place my finger into the mark of the nails, and place my hand to his side, I will never believe.*"[83] Wow. That's pretty strong. Thomas not only would require visual confirmation, he would have to physically touch the wounds of Jesus in order to believe. Pretty tough cookie, maybe.

I wonder, though, if he was just *really* disappointed. Perhaps he was deeply and desperately discouraged by the death of Jesus, the end of the dream team. I suspect Thomas may have felt the death of Christ and the subsequent floundering in a way that threatened to derail his faith.

82 Matthew 9:35, 36
83 Ibid., v. 25

But Jesus knew that. He was intimately acquainted with all of his men, including the-glass-is-always-half-empty Thomas, who is a little like Eeyore. Which kind of makes me want to dismiss him. But Jesus did not.

Jesus stepped outside of Himself and entered the experience of Thomas. Jesus was committed to His friend. He made a repeat appearance primarily for the benefit of Eeyore … I mean, Thomas. Not only did He show up, He knew exactly what Thomas had said that he would need, *and He gave it to him!* I know this is my un-empathetic womanhood speaking, but seriously? O my, I love this Savior.

"Put your finger here, and see my hands; and put out your hand, and place it in my side. Do not disbelieve, but believe."[84] I recently saw the previews for a new movie being released this spring about the life of Christ. (Interesting, how Hollywood keeps making this movie.) The preview shows this exact scene, and as Jesus lifts His hand to touch His friend, there is an actual hole in His hand. You can see right through it. Perhaps that's why this story is so fresh in my mind. I saw the hole on the big screen. Thomas saw it in the flesh, or lack thereof.

The *ESV Study Bible* describes what follows as Thomas' "clear confession of his newly found faith in Jesus as His Lord and God."[85] That text goes on to say that Thomas' confession is one of the strongest references in the New Testament on the deity of Christ. Which was for our benefit, and the benefit of the thousands and thousands of people throughout the ages who would not see that hole but who would believe.

Jesus knew that Thomas, in particular of the twelve, was harassed and helpless. He felt compassion for his friend. He did

84 Ibid, v. 27
85 *ESV Study Bible* notes on John 20:28

not chastise him or lecture him or throw him out. He entered into his suffering and rescued him. Doesn't that make you sigh with gratitude?

Sympathy Is not Empathy

You are perhaps familiar with the author of Hebrews' treatise on Jesus' empathy with all humanity. That text reads: *"For we do not have a high priest who is unable to sympathize with our weaknesses, but one who in every respect has been tempted as we are, yet without sin."*[86]

Here, the author deploys the Greek version of our Hebrew *nacham.* The Greek, *sumpatheo*, is only used twice in Scripture – both times in this letter to the Hebrews. It means "to be affected with the same feeling as another; to feel for, have compassion on." God, in Christ, empathizes with human experience not just by *knowing* about it, but also by actually entering into it. Skip Moen, author of the blog *Hebrew Word Study* says:

"Yeshua [Jesus] shares our experience. He doesn't share an experience *similar* to ours. He shares our *exact* experience. In fact, He is the only one able to understand exactly what we are experiencing because He knows everything we feel, do, think and say."[87]

This is the ultimate expression of empathy. In an article titled "Are You Suffering from Empathy Deficit Disorder" by Douglas LaBier, the author describes the difference between sympathy and empathy. He suggests that "sympathy" is the ability to understand another's situation through your own lens, creating your own version of their story. Empathy, alter-

86 Hebrews 4:15
87 "In This Together," *Hebrew Word Study* November 8, 2009

natively, is the stepping outside of self and entering the world, the experience, of the other person.

Compassion, sympathy and empathy all have to do with *feeling*, but true empathy – the kind that God demonstrates as He *helps* humanity by giving us Jesus – goes one step further. It *enters into*. Through Jesus, God is revealed as the One who helps with the capacity to enter into human experience and the power and commitment to actively do so. This is the Philippians 2 principle: "*Have this mind among yourselves, which is yours in Christ Jesus, who, though he was in the form of God, did not count equality with God a thing to be grasped, but made himself nothing, taking the form of a servant, being born in the likeness of men. And being found in human form* [entering into!], *he humbled himself by becoming obedient to the point of death, even death on a cross.*"[88]

Sympathy would not be enough to save us. In His incarnation, we see the *ezer* image of God as He stoops to empathize, to feel compassion for, and enter into our suffering and shame. It is, until His death and resurrection, the greatest act of empathy, *nacham*, in human history.

The Lost Art of Empathy

As we have perused the pages of Scripture, we have seen the *helper* nature of God as He pitied and comforted His servant David. We have seen this *ezer*-God in the empathetic heart of His only Son, who "suffered into" Thomas' grief and disappointment and helped him. We see the Savior's ultimate act of empathy as He not only <u>felt</u> our pain but also willingly entered into it at the ultimate cost of His own life. Finally, the *ezer* empathizer

88 Philippians 2

God expresses *nacham* as He sends the *parakletos*, the Comforter, to be an ever-present *help* so that we would not be alone.

Why then do I, a Christ-follower, have so much trouble empathizing?

In 1946 during the Nuremberg tribunals, the U.S. Army assigned Dr. Gustav M. Gilbert, a psychologist fluent in German, to study the minds and motivations of the Nazi defendants. The following year, his *Nuremberg Diary* was published, containing transcripts of his conversations with the prisoners. It is recorded that during the trials Gilbert told the Head Prosecutor: "I told you once that I was searching for the nature of evil. I think I've come close to defining it: a lack of empathy. It's the one characteristic that connects all the defendants: a genuine incapacity to feel with their fellow man. *Evil, I think, is the absence of empathy.*"[89]

That seems extreme, doesn't it? It makes me uncomfortable and I want to believe that such a characterization is limited to people like those Nazi defendants. Unfortunately, that's not the case.

Curious, I Googled "a perpetrator's lack of empathy" to determine whether Gilbert's assessment of the Nuremberg defendants has a more current application in our culture. The first ten links that presented themselves each referenced sex offenders. With titles such as "Sexual Offender Empathy Deficits" and "Guilt and Shame with Regards to Sex Offender Empathy" it quickly became evident that a lack of empathy has some dramatic role to play in a person's ability to purposefully cause sexual harm to another person.

Continuing the search, an empathy deficit is cited in cases of

89 *Nuremberg Diary,* Dr. Gustav M. Gilbert

domestic abuse, cyber-bullying, school violence, animal abuse, and hazing. Whether the lack of empathy is genetic and/or a learned coping mechanism is under debate. Regardless, the apparent absence of empathy is an unhappy epidemic in our modern society.

Douglas LaBier agrees. "EDD [Empathy Deficit Disorder] is more severe than ever," he writes. "When you suffer from it you're unable to step outside yourself and tune in to what other people experience, especially those who feel, think and believe differently from yourself. That makes it a source of personal conflicts, of communication ... EDD keeps you locked inside a self-centered world."[90]

The absence of empathy is not the exclusive domain of Nazi war criminals, or sex offenders, or frat boys who perpetrate agony on their recruits. I "suffer" from EDD. Actually, it seems more accurate to say that *others suffer from my EDD.*

This is true even in the church. Instead of empathizing, feeling compassion, and affinity, we judge. We judge women who work outside of the home – or women who choose to stay at home. We judge women who homeschool their children – or women who choose to send their children to private or public school. We judge women who live in big houses – or women who live on the "other side" of town. We judge women who bottle feed, use disposable diapers, put their babies on a schedule, or not. EDD.

The Genesis of EDD

What LaBier fails to acknowledge is that Scripture, while

90 "Are You Suffering from EDD?", Douglas LaBier PhD, www.psychologytoday.com

liberally expounding on the *ezer-empathizer* nature of God, speaks also to my deficiency. The first evidence of it is seen just pages into our original history. Genesis 4 describes man's first murder as Cain took the life of his brother, Abel, feeling no empathy for Abel or for his parents as he killed and buried their second son. Thus began a legacy of heartless, self-centered relational dynamics that plagued the people of God for centuries.

Remember Sarai, "dealing harshly" with Hagar and sending her off into the wilderness? What about Shechem "defiling" Dinah? (A little obscure, I know.) Or the abandonment of Joseph by his brothers, who tried to kill him but failed? And we're just 37 chapters into the first book of the Bible.

The empathy deficit problem – this refusal to think about the needs, the emotion, the circumstances of others – was addressed in some form or fashion by the prophets and the Apostles, in almost every era of the faith.

EDD. Not a condition that I "find myself in," but one that is painfully inherent in my old nature. I am, at least to a degree, just like Sarai. And Shechem. And Joseph's plotting brothers. I am uninterested in the trauma happening in Haiti. I am critical and condescending of those who become paralyzed by their suffering. I avoid getting personally involved in the heartache of others. I do not climb into their skin or walk in their shoes not because I *can't.* But because I *won't.* My heart is *desperately wicked.*

The "disorder" of empathy is, sadly, in our fallen DNA. In LaBier's language, we are "locked inside our self-centered world." Left to ourselves, we will not exercise our capacity to think about the needs, the emotion, and the circumstances of others. It's too messy. Too time-consuming. Too draining.

What's an *ezer* to do?

A Faith-filled Disposition

By the grace of God, we will not lose heart. Our uniquely feminine disposition flows out of our faith. While our sinful nature promotes a self-protective, distracted disinterest in the needs of others, this is not our experience of God. Informed by the psalms, and texts such as Philippians 2 and Hebrews 4, we grow in our faith, which overflows into a disposition to be women who bear the *ezer-empathizer* image of God. The Gospel forces me to see others and myself differently. More like Christ.

As I think about my life with God, I am often undone by the fact that He "sympathizes with my weakness." That He is not surprised by my failure, annoyed by my repeated faithlessness or uninterested in my heartache actually makes me weep.

There have been several seasons in my life, as I consider them in hindsight, during which the image of the Good Shepherd picking up that wayward sheep and gently bringing him or her back to the safety of the sheepfold is particularly poignant.

I am that sheep. I wander from the flock. I am enamored by the world. I want my own way. I don't want to live with the other sheep. They annoy me. Worse, I don't really want the Shepherd. I mostly want to be left alone.

Hymn writer Robert Robinson penned these words that capture my own heart: "Prone to wander, Lord I feel it. Prone to leave the God I love."[91]

But my Shepherd will not turn away. He will not give up. He *nacham,* is moved to pity, to compassion. By His death and resurrection, He has entered into my suffering and shame, but He will not leave me there. He *empathizes* and helps and comes after me.

91 "Come Thou Fount of Every Blessing," Robert Robinson

Oh that my disposition would more resemble His.

Remembering

Several months ago I sat with Gina[92], a single friend, over lunch. She had been in a small group with me for two years during which time she had come to saving faith and grown to love God with a deep and abiding passion which had in turn birthed an affection for the church. What a delight to see all that God had done and to look forward with her to the future.

The only problem was David.[93] They had been together since college and she loved him. But his own lack of interest in spiritual things, his resistance to the Gospel and his dismissal of Scripture worried her. She had so hoped he would "come around." But so far she had seen no leaning toward God. No redemptive curiosity. She was seriously considering whether to end the relationship, but the thought of doing so was agonizing.

As I listened to her, we both cried. While it has been more than thirty years ago, I vividly remember my own heartache over the growing chasm between my love for God and my love for the man in my life. I knew that I would have to choose and, when I chose the Lord and lost the man, it was as if someone reached in and pulled my heart out of my chest. I actually ached. I cried for days ... weeks.

The beauty of the church, however, is the gift of shared experience and history. God's absolute faithfulness and the unwavering reality of His steadfast love to me as I navigated that heartache became, for Gina, a life line to hang onto during the days and weeks ahead in her own journey. Because I was able to *remember* – because I had actually been in her skin and walked

92 Not her real name
93 Not his real name

around in it – I was able to empathize. To *nacham*. To pity, to console, to have compassion.

By faith, the *ezer* woman of God remembers her own experience and does not stand far off from people who are hurting. She comforts. She consoles. She steps outside of herself and enters into their world as she recalls her own history, and she moves toward them.

This is the principle that Paul exhorts in his second letter to the Corinthian church. 2 Corinthians 1:4 says *"the Father… comforts us in all our affliction* **so that we may be able to comfort those who are in any affliction, with the comfort with which we ourselves are comforted by God.**" O my, I love that. To at least some degree, the purpose of my heartbreak in 1982 was so that I would *remember the faithfulness of God* and share it with Gina. In 2013.

So I remember what it was like to be young and in love.

I remember what it was like to miscarry a baby when I was 16 weeks pregnant.

I remember what it was like to mother a wandering son.

I remember what it was like to lose my father. Suddenly.

I remember what it was like to have an "empty nest." Wow, the house was quiet.

I remember what it was like to love my sin more than my Savior. (Yesterday.)

I have lived more than 50 years. For at least 35 of those years, I have walked with God. Though I have wandered, He has never failed me. I want so much to have the disposition of an *ezer* helper who remembers my own experience of God, empathizing with others and entering into their experience with the truth of

God's faithfulness as our hope.

Remember.

It's Czech to Me

Several years ago our family traveled to Prague over the holiday to visit my son who was taking a gap year in Europe. He had been living in Prague for several months and had become quite savvy in the city.

If you have never been to the Czech Republic, or seen the Czech language on a street sign, you may not know how completely foreign it feels. There are 42 letters in the Czech alphabet, and some are "backwards" (from the English version!) and some have accent marks above them. Which is no help to me at all. The combinations of letters seem nonsensical. Like *jdete*. Which means walk. How do you pronounce a word with a "j" and a "d" together?

I'm told that Czech is native to about 12 million people. Somehow, Milas picked up enough of the language to make his way around and to communicate with many of the locals. Me? I've never felt like the foreigner as much as I did in Prague. Street signs, subway station markings, restaurant menus, grocery store labels. I had no frame of reference. Beautiful city. Lovely people. Cra*zy* language.

Sometimes experiencing another person's condition, or being aware of their thoughts and feelings is particularly difficult because you have no frame of reference. Their experience is so foreign to you that you don't even know how to begin to understand.

This has been the case often in my friendships with single women. These sisters, some of whom are over 40, have endured many years of disappointment, hurt, confusion, discouragement, and despair. Most live in light of the Gospel and their typical experience is of God's kindness and love, but they have each had moments ... days ... weeks ... seasons ... of sorrow.

I cannot begin to understand their circumstances. I have been married to the love of my life since I was 20 years old. I can count the number of nights that I have slept in our bed alone. Every single major life event we have experienced together. Unless the Lord intervenes, I anticipate this being the ongoing story of my remaining years this side of heaven.

This disparity of experience, while challenging, does not hinder my ability to empathize with my friends. I ask a lot of questions and I do a lot of listening. I work hard not to assume. I go out of my way to engage in their world and to invite them into mine. In these relationships where we don't have much in common the key to a growing *ezer* disposition is in doing the hard work of seeking to understand. It is in actually *learning the language.*

The writer of Proverbs puts it this way: "*The purpose in a man's heart is like deep water, but a man of understanding will draw it out.*" [94] Jesus was a master of drawing out a man's heart. Remember his discussion with the woman of Samaria? That interaction could have been much more abbreviated, saving the Lord's time for more important things. Instead, Jesus asked her one question after another, listening to her answers until she stood there, quite exposed. Granted, Jesus did not deploy this method so that He would understand what was going on in her heart – He clearly knew what was there. But *she* needed to know. So He asked. And asked. And asked. Then He was able to give her the Living Water, which she so desperately craved.

How am I to empathize with people who are not at all like

94 Proverbs 20:5

me, whose lives are different in every way from mine, whose history has no parallel to my history?

Ask questions. Listen more than I talk. Seek to understand. Learn the language.

You're a Mean One …

During the holiday, I watched (for the millionth time) "How the Grinch Stole Christmas." And I thought, "that's me." My heart really is that small. I am, perhaps, the most non-empathetic person that I know. I do not want to be bothered by the needs of others and, when confronted by them, I am condescending and judgmental.

But God is pressing in on my small heart. As I've put the words down on these pages, I am sobered by my forgetfulness. Hebrews 4, in particular, has resonated in my heart and mind for weeks – that Jesus would leave heaven and come *here*, to this world full of hatred and ugliness and failure and sickness, entering into my experience so that He could "help me in struggle and comfort me in sorrow"[95] is truly more than I can comprehend. He has *helped me and comforted me.* He has shown compassion on me, the afflicted. He took the form of a servant, made Himself nothing so that He could walk in my skin – and then rescue me from it. This is the theology that informs my womanhood.

I don't know that my heart has grown three sizes, but I know that God is growing me up. I want to live in light of the great empathy of God in Christ for me. I want that *nacham* to become the familiar beat of my own heart as I engage with the people in my little world, and I pray for those far away.

95 Spurgeon, *Treasury of David*

As with the "H" in our acrostic, the disposition of empathy is costly. At the moment when the capacity for empathy crosses over into the activity of actually walking in someone else's shoes, there is a price to be paid. The woman who reflects the *ezer* image of God will part with something as trivial as time, or something as significant as her personal, closely held biases. She will not be unchanged.

In his Gospel, Matthew describes the baptism of Jesus by John the Baptist.[96] One has to wonder why Jesus, the Messiah, the Son of God needed to be baptized. John wondered that, too. Jesus explained, at least partially, *"Thus it is fitting for us to fulfill all righteousness."* Jesus' baptism would serve to fulfill the prophecies of the Old Testament. But this baptism was more than a connection to the past. It was the launching of His earthly ministry and a visible picture of the Savior's identifying with the sinful people whom He had come to save.[97] He's climbing into their skin.

Which is pretty stunning. But do you know what happened next? Immediately following Matthew's account of Jesus' baptism, His actively identifying with humanity, we read these words: *"Then Jesus was led up by the Spirit into the wilderness to be tempted by the devil."* Jesus "put on human skin" and walked around in it. He shared an experience not *similar* to ours, but actually much more excruciating. His "entering into" came with a very high price tag. Why should I expect anything less?

"He ... made Himself nothing, taking the form of a servant, being born in the likeness of men. And being found in human form, He humbled Himself by becoming obedient to the point of death, even death on a cross."

96 Matthew 3:13-17
97 ESV study notes on the text

This is the theology of the "E" in my helper disposition. He has empathized with me, entered into my shame and suffering, and He rescued me. This is my creation design. I am made to be an empathizer. This is Christ in me, the display of God's redemptive grace in my *ezer* disposition.

I recently returned from a trip to Haiti during which I visited the epicenter of the earthquake in a city called Legone on the fourth anniversary of that devastating disaster. I had the incredible opportunity to actually see with my own eyes what I had previously only seen through technology. I held a sleeping child, orphaned by the earthquake's devastation, while his friends played the largest game of duck-duck-goose that I've ever seen, and I looked at his little shoes with new perspective. Having actually *been there*, now I see Haiti through the eyes of the orphans and I am overwhelmed with compassion. I *nacham*.

Empathy. What will it take for such compassion to overflow from me to my family? To my neighbors? To my churchmen? What will it take?

Chapter Six

TWO ARE BETTER THAN ONE

"L" is for "Lifter"

During my first fifteen years on staff at our church, I had served two Senior Pastors. The first had been called to our little church plant in its very early days. His transfer to another church after almost twenty years was challenging, but the appointment of his Senior Associate Pastor to the role of Senior Pastor promised an exciting and hopeful season for our staff and congregation and we enjoyed a relatively smooth transition. When that man made the difficult decision to resign just two short years later, our church was catapulted into a challenging and painful year characterized by dissension, discouragement, and fear. The summer of 2006 was perhaps the most agonizing of my professional ministry life. With the exception of the death of my dad, it was arguably the most difficult season of my personal spiritual journey.

During that summer, many of my friends and most of my family members who had been engaged in ministry with me for years left our church. Almost weekly I would learn of another family who had given up. We had a series of retired ministers who filled our pulpit and several who served for some months to lead our staff. Of the seven pastors on our staff at the time, six of them left over the course of eighteen months. It was heartbreaking.

I can remember going about my own job with something like stoic determination. I was personally so crushed by the events surrounding me that I just put my head down and tried to do my job. I felt the weight of my role as I carefully guarded my words and kept my deep disappointment to myself. But on the inside I was crumbling. I cried out to the Lord and begged Him to let me leave. I felt very much like I was suffocating, and I did not know how long I could last. Worship was dry and empty. Well, more likely it was *me* that was dry and empty; the state of my soul could not be fixed by one hour in worship, even with the best of interim preachers.

Even as I recall those days to put the words on paper, I find myself cringing. It was awful. I desperately needed perspective. I needed encouragement. I needed hope. I needed Truth.

We have considered the faith-filled disposition of a *helper*, designed by God and made in His *ezer* image, as she cultivates and tends a **H**edge of protection around the people in her care. We have seen her uniquely feminine disposition demonstrate itself in her **E**mpathy for others, "climbing into their skin" and seeking to understand what may be unfamiliar to her.

Having seen others' disappointment, fear and discouragement, the *helper* discovers the third characteristic of the *ezer* image of God that applies to womanhood: it is her *response* as she longs to **L**ift others out of the miry pit of misery. It is a difficult proposition, messy and often costly. However, her own experience of God's *help* in the valley informs her ability and inflames her passion to bring confidence and hope to people like me, suffocating with despair. Unfortunately, in the summer of 2006, it seemed like I was on my own.

Rehab Addict

A house cannot stand without columns. I'm not talking about the columns that characterize beautiful plantation houses or stately sprawling mansions. I'm talking about columns that are integral to the structure of every house, vertical posts that hold the entire structure and protect it from "lateral disintegration"[98] – in layman's terms that means "falling down."

There's a series on one of the home improvement networks that chronicles projects undertaken by a woman who purchases and rehabs old homes. One issue that is common to every project is the soundness of the foundation and the "bones," or the structure of the home. Replacing the tile and restoring the cabinets are costly wastes of time and resources if the structure is not sound, so crumbling foundations and weak columns are an early priority.

Perhaps this is what the psalmist had in mind as he penned these words about the *helper-ezer* God, *"Behold, God is my ezer; the Lord is the upholder of my life."*[99] The Hebrew word used here for "upholder" is *camak*. It means, "to lean against, to support or sustain." It is used eleven times in the psalms and it is the same word used for our word "column." The setting for this particular occasion is thought to be 1 Samuel 23, a familiar scene in the life of David.

Saul is hunting the young, soon-to-be king. Again. The Scripture actually says, *"Saul sought him every day."* " Every single day. But the second half of that verse may have been the basis for David's claim of God, His *helper-upholder: "Saul sought him every day, but God did not give him into his hand."*[100] Again, we turn to Spurgeon, who comments on this text: "He saw his enemies everywhere, and now, to his joy...he sees One whose aid is better than the help of all men."[101]

David understood the *ezer* nature of God, that it was God

98 www.column.ezinemark.com
99 Psalm 54:4
100 I Samuel 23:14
101 Spurgeon, *Treasury of David*

who would sustain him, uphold him, **LIFT** him out of the pit and snare of danger. It would not be his armies and chariots and weapons that would keep him from lateral disintegration. It would be His *upholder-ezer,* God.

Woe Is Me

When my sister and I were in middle school, we had the opportunity to perform together in a school play. I have no idea what part I played, but I remember Leslie's role. She played the part of a household maid and her only line – which she repeated with some melodrama each time she came on stage – was "Woe is me!" Her acting became more dramatic with each successive appearance, as the audience roared with laughter.

The psalms resonate with "woe is me," the written litany of the troubles of God's people. Psalms that articulate personal hardship are called "psalms of lament" and, as categories go, they represent the largest single category of psalms in the Psalter. Among the psalms of lament are 3, 6, 12, 13, 28, 44, 56, 60, 74, 79, 80, 83, and 85…. You get the picture. These painfully honest psalms describe the author's anger, his depression, his frustration, his disappointment, his fatigue, his fear, and his loneliness. He is sometimes describing his own personal journey; other occasions articulate the corporate experience of the people of Israel.

The most amazing thread that weaves together the majority of the psalms of lament, however, is the ultimate concluding confidence that we have already seen in Psalm 54. *"Behold, God is my ezer, the Lord is the upholder of my life."* God, who will in due time save His people, does, in the meantime, sustain them, and lift them up.[102]

102 Matthew Henry's Commentary, Psalm 54

Psalm 20:2 is another occasion of the *ezer-upholder* God helping His people. This little verse sits in the midst of a song written for use by the people of God on the occasion of a national crisis. The first five verses are to be sung by the people to the king as they voice their hope in the Lord on the eve of battle. Tucked into that text is this verse, *"May He send you ezer from the sanctuary and give you support from Zion."* These words illustrate a principle unique to the nation of Israel among all the other nations: their leader was not surrounded by a mighty military. Instead, the king of Israel served in the shadow of the majestic figure of Yahweh. It was God who would **LIFT** them out of their national crisis. It was God who would rescue and preserve them. Not their armory. Not their treasury. Not their princes. Their rescue and preservation came instead from their sanctuary. The context of verse 2 declares the psalmist's confidence in God's protection, His support, His faithfulness, and His strength. How will God *ezer* His people? He will support them – hold them up, lift them and give them strength.

Psalm 18:35 *"You have given me the shield of salvation and your right hand supported me."*

Psalm 94:18 *"When my foot slips, your steadfast love, O Lord, held me up..."*

Psalm 119:17 *"Hold me up, that I may be safe..."*

Psalm 145:14 *"The Lord upholds all that fall..."*

I heard a version of these psalms as I stood beside hundreds of Haitian Christians at that church service on the fourth anniversary of the 2010 earthquake. "Be strong in the Lord and in the strength of His might," their Pastor cried out. To which the people, those who lived among the 150,000 who died, replied "*Merci, Seigneur.*" Thank you, God. The lament of their excruciating loss was concluded by their confidence in the God who **LIFTS**. The One who holds up the heartbroken so that they will not be crushed.

To the psalmist who cries, "Woe is me," God is sufficient. He that upholds all things by His grace will, likewise, hold up His people. Much like the strong, solid column that provides stability for the structure of an aging home, the *ezer-helper* God is "He that upholds my [sagging] soul, and keeps me from tiring in my work and sinking under my burdens."[103] What a relief!

The Thread of Helper-Lifter Theology

The psalms are the oasis in the desert of human experience. They are full of promises of God's presence, His power and His help. But there is a wider Biblical witness to the theology of God our Helper who is our Lifter, our support. 1 Kings 19 describes a surprising circumstance in the life of the great prophet Elijah.

Elijah was a hero in his day among God's people. He boldly spoke the Word of the Lord and his reputation as a man of God was confirmed by miracles like the multiplying of one widow's oil and the raising of another's son from the dead. He reached the pinnacle of his prophetic career, however, on the crest of Mount Carmel. This is where the Lord soundly defeated the prophets of Baal through Elijah's word. The forty-six verses that describe this battle between Yahweh and the impotent god, Baal, portray an epic scene that has stirred the hearts of men for generations. At the end, when *"the heavens grew black with clouds and wind, and there was a great rain. And Ahab rode and went to Jezreel. And the hand of the Lord was on*

103 ibid.

Elijah, and he gathered up his garment and ran before Ahab," even the most passive listener should be moved to some great show of enthusiastic emotion. "GO, ELIJAH, GO!"

Now skip down just three verses. Ahab had run to his wicked wife and whined to her about his humiliating loss. She was raging with fury. At Elijah. And Elijah was afraid. *"Then he was afraid, and he arose and ran for his life."* Wow. What a disappointment. Is our great hero in reality a chicken?

Not really. Actually, I suspect Elijah was exhausted. The next eighteen verses describe a man who was weary. And lonely. And discouraged. And confused. So he ran away to the desert and took a nap.

And then the Lord showed up. He who upholds all things by His provident grace kept His man from sinking under his burdens. Elijah found himself fed by the hand of God for many days and nights. The Word of the Lord came to him and strengthened him, sustaining him and lifting him up. He was for Elijah the pillar that prevented the prophet's lateral disintegration. Elijah would go on to boldly and faithfully serve the Lord.

The New Testament bears witness to the *helper-lifter* nature of God in Christ as His ministry is marked by the hope-filled restoration of sight to the blind, mobility to the lame, and vitality to the sick.

I recently heard a Christian speaker who was expounding on the story of Jesus and the sick man by the pool of Bethesda from John 5. It was said that this particular pool had healing water that occasionally "stirred up," and when it did, those who were in the water would be healed. The man who encountered the Savior that day had been lying by that pool for thirty-eight years. Thirty-eight years. Scripture does not say exactly what was wrong with him, only that he was an invalid. When Jesus saw the man lying there, He asked the invalid: *"Do you want to be healed?"*[104] The man's reply revealed a pretty lonely and limited existence, as he told Jesus that he had no one to put him into the water when it stirred. What may be implied by his response is that he was totally incapable of getting himself even close to the water. He could not help himself.

When the speaker got to this point in her talk, she suggested emphatically that the man must not have wanted to be healed very badly for, if he wanted to be healed, surely over the course of thirty-eight years he would have found a way to inch himself closer to the pool! Her point was that, if we want something from God, we would do well to prove how much we want it and to do whatever is in our power to bring it about.

Except that the *precise point* of this story is the helplessness and hopelessness of this man's plight. He did not move closer to the pool because *he could not* and because *no one would help him*. To mock the invalid, to suggest that he just did not want it badly enough is to mitigate the power of the Gospel here. This man needed JESUS to lift him out of his helpless condition. He needed the *ezer-lifter* Son of God to hold him up, to support him, to give him a hope and a future. Without Christ, the man by the Bethesda pool would have died there.

This visible demonstration illustrates the message that Jesus would preach throughout His earthly ministry. His clear declaration of truth and bold revelation of sin lifted followers from their deep depravity to the promise of life everlasting. The thread of sustaining grace that illustrates the psalmist's confidence in God's promise to *send help from Zion* is evident on every page of every Gospel account of Jesus' ministry. The upholding of life while He walked among us would lead, ultimately, to

104 John 5:6

the Savior's lifting His elect from death to life through the glory of the cross and the power of His resurrection. *"What is sown is perishable; what is raised is imperishable. It is sown in dishonor; it is raised in glory. It is sown in weakness; it is raised in power."*[105]

This is fallen humanity in disrepair without the prospect of renovation lifted and renewed at its very core, its bones. What was perishable is now forever. What was scandalous is now full of splendor. What was feeble is now strong. Hallelujah, what a Savior!

Life Is Hard

I have a friend whose house was sagging. Not her physical house; that one is actually a two-story colonial on a cul-de-sac in a nearby neighborhood that has been beautifully updated. The sagging structure was the "house" that was her life. She had been married for eight years and they had been hoping for a baby for five years. She had not been able to become pregnant and they had tried fertilization meds, other procedures and finally, twice unsuccessfully, in vitro fertilization. She was just over thirty and her comment over coffee put her experience into perspective: "I feel like I'm being lapped," she sighed. "All of my friends have had their first baby and most are either pregnant or have had a second child. I feel like I'm just being left in their dust."

To which I replied, "You *are* being lapped. That's a fair observation. It's not just a feeling; it's a fact." A reply that, admittedly, may not seem very empathetic. You are probably thinking that I need to read chapter 5 of this book again, which might not be a bad idea. But the reality is that sometimes life is just hard. There are many occasions in our lives that remind us that, to a great degree, we do not have control of our world and things happen to us that are painful. Much like the formerly grand home that

105 1 Corinthians 15:42-44

has been assailed by the elements, our lives are often subject to the harsh onslaught of heartache. We are sad. And discouraged. And exhausted by…

The accidental death of a friend's father in a car accident caused by a drunk driver.

The leukemia that rages in the little tiny body of a young couple's 14-month-old baby.

The economic impact of the closing of a local textile plant.

The demise of a friend's marriage that she fought hard to save.

We live in a culture that celebrates self-reliance. We are independent, and we have a "can-do" attitude. Which is great. Except there are some things in life that we just can't do. No matter how hard we try, how much money we spend, or how much education we get. We cannot always "have it our way," in spite of the savvy advertising slogan. Life is hard.

Which did not surprise Jesus, and it should not have surprised his disciples. We have already seen Him warn them that it would be so. *"In the world you will have tribulation."*[106] Notice the declarative nature of that statement. Jesus did not suggest that perhaps his friends would struggle. He advised them bluntly: Get ready. You *will* have trouble. Life is hard.

And it was. Having been gripped by the Gospel, these men lost their homes, their livelihood, their friends and families. Most of the original twelve disciples of Jesus served Him faithfully in the new church, until each was martyred for his faith. While Scripture records only the violent deaths of John the Baptist[107] and James,[108] history reveals that all but John,

106 John 16:33
107 Matthew 14:1-12; Mark 6:14-29; Luke 9:7-9
108 Acts 12:1, 2

the brother of James, lost their lives for the sake of the Gospel. Beheaded, speared to death, and crucified, these men had followed Christ even after full disclosure. Hardship was part of the bargain.

I Will Never Live This Down

Some years ago I traveled with a team of volunteers to Charleston, South Carolina. Charleston is our family's refuge from real life; we have been vacationing on the beach there since the children were babies.

One evening we headed to town for dinner. We were loaded into three vans, and I was in the lead vehicle because I was familiar with the route. We had no GPS and no cell phones, but each van did have a walkie-talkie, and a "handle" [code name]. We thought we were very high tech.

I'm not sure if it was the darkness or the distraction of eight women in the van, or just my momentary lapse of sanity, but somehow we found ourselves going the wrong way on a one-way street. With both vans following close behind. As the driver of our van realized what we had done, I tried to yell into the walkie-talkie, "Don't follow us! Don't follow us!" The second van had already made the turn and was just behind us. The third driver was able to heed the warning.

The Lord kindly protected all three vans and no one was hurt. We arrived at the restaurant trembling with relief.

Now we laugh at that story. Well, *they* laugh. I have a charm on my silver bracelet that is a "one way" sign, a gift from one of the passengers in the lead van. Just so I won't ever forget.

I have used this story on multiple occasions to teach some biblical principle – like "be careful whom you are following."

Or "the humbling exercise of leadership."

I use it here for another reason. As I have thought about that evening, and that moment when we took the wrong turn, one that I had *never* taken before and in very familiar territory, I realize that I had somehow lost my perspective. I could not think fast enough to figure out where we were and where we needed to be. The darkness, the chatter, the pressure to get it right. I completely lost my perspective.

That happens in the dark, doesn't it? The things that we are so certain of in the light of day somehow lose their surety in the terrifying blackness of night. We, like the prophet Elijah and my baby-less friend, are unable to find our way and the promises to which we would usually cling have disappeared like a vapor in the wind.

As I write these words, my mother lies in the next room, slowly dying of cancer. It's excruciating. She is confined to her bed, unable to read or do much for herself, and her memory is fading.

My mom is one of the godliest women that I have ever known. She has been a powerful influence in our own family. I have had the privilege to sit under her teaching for many years, first as a Bible Study Fellowship teaching leader, then as a teacher in my own church. She has mentored dozens of women, many of whom continue to visit at her bedside, longing for her assuring counsel.

But this has been a tremendously challenging season for my mother's faith. She *knows* what is true, but oh how easy it is to forget. John Bunyan aptly described this season for us: "This valley is a very solitary place. A wilderness, a land of deserts, and of pits; a land of drought, and of the shadow of death."[109] My mother knows that God has a plan for her, to bless her and to prosper her.[110] She knows that His purpose will prevail. She knows that all things work together for good to those who love God and are called according to His purpose. She knows that He loves her with an everlasting love, that He will never leave her nor forsake her, that His ways are higher than our ways…

And yet, after almost fourteen weeks of being in bed, when she opens her eyes every morning to the familiar sights of her window, and bookcase, and rocking chair, she forgets. And she weeps for another day *not* in heaven. And so do I.

Perspective. We are, as Spurgeon would say, doing business in great waters and we long to see His wonders in the deep.[111] But mostly we're drowning, gasping for air, and treading water.

God Helps Those Who Help Themselves

Old fashioned sword drill. Find this verse in the Bible: "God helps those who help themselves." GO! … .. Pages are swooshing as women look in their concordance for a clue, flipping to a verse that is close, but no. Where is it? Keeeeep looking…. Until in frustration, one of the women declares, "I don't think it's in here!" Bingo. It's not in there.

"God helps those who help themselves" has become a phrase that we toss around as if it is Scripture. But it's not. That phrase is an American moralistic aphorism that we have tried to spiritualize. Which is worrisome, since that line of thinking is exactly the opposite of the Gospel. God actually helps those

109 *The Pilgrim's Progress*, p. 66
110 It is instructive to note that Jeremiah wrote these words in the *midst* of Israel's suffering.
111 *Morning and Evening*, Deuteronomy 5:24

who *cannot help themselves*. Like Elijah. And the invalid man by the pool of Bethesda. And my mom. This is what Paul writes about in Romans 8: *"God has done what the law, weakened by the flesh could not do."*[112] Christ came to die for sinners who could not save themselves.

Such is my *ezer-lifting* experience of God. The summer of 2006 did not end as it began. It was a very dark and wearisome season with one day dragging into another as I navigated my own disappointment. The one "bright spot" during those weeks was the Bible study that I shared with eight or nine good friends in the comfort of my mother's den. We were studying the psalms of ascent, reading Eugene Peterson's *A Long Obedience in the Same Direction*. These have become some of my most favorite chapters in all of Scripture, but I have particular affection for Psalm 126. I don't know what happened in my soul when we got to this chapter in our study, but something "clicked." I read and meditated on these words:

"When the Lord restored the fortunes of Zion, we were like those who dream. Then our mouth was filled with laughter and our tongue with shouts of joy; then they said among the nations, 'The Lord has done great things for them.' The Lord has done great things for us; we are glad. Restore our fortunes, O Lord, like streams in the Negeb! Those who sow in tears shall reap with shouts of joy! He who goes out weeping, bearing the seed for sowing, shall come home with shouts of joy, bringing his sheaves with him."

I began to consider all of the "great things" that the Lord had done for our church, and for me, in particular. I made a list that was *pages* long and I was overwhelmed with hope and gratitude. Literally overnight, my soul was convinced that we would be like the Israelites. That one day, some day, our mouths would be

112 Romans 8:3

filled with laughter again and our tongue with shouts of joy. I believed that God would restore our fortunes. Such confidence gave me the capacity to stay the course, and to do so with hope.

Which is not to say that I went to work the next day and all was well. The laughing and shouting was noticeably absent. Still, something in me was different. Even over the next year or two, during which we called a new Senior Pastor and set out on a new journey of ministry, we continued to watch the exodus of friends and ministry partners – but my commitment to and affection for our church has *never wavered*. God literally lifted me out of spiritual depression and gave me during those days a deep and abiding sense of hope and joy that has characterized the past seven years of my personal and ministry life and I've had the privilege to enjoy many days of laughter. God has restored our fortunes and we are "bringing in the sheaves." *Many* new friends have joined us in worship and in work. I am *so grateful.*

I was a mess that summer. I could not have helped myself if you had given me a manual with illustrated instructions. What a relief to be *lifted* by the *ezer* God through the power of His Word, held up and supported by the One who called me to Himself and set me on this path.

A Faith-filled Disposition

There is an obscure detail in the Old Testament story of the prophet Jeremiah's rescue from the cistern. In Jeremiah 38, we find the prophet at the bottom of a well, sinking in the mud, having been thrown there by his enemies and left for dead. Verse 6 says *"And Jeremiah sank in the mud."* Jeremiah, on his own, was a goner.

But this prophet had friends (which, if you remember your prophet history, is a bit unique ... these weren't the most popular guys on the block). Jeremiah's friends set out to rescue him. They found a really long rope and made plans to lower it into the well. But before they did so, the Scripture tells us that Ebed-melech (that's Jeremiah's friend) tied rags and worn out clothes to the rope. He called down to Jeremiah that the rope was coming and gave him this instruction: *"put the rags and clothes between your armpits and the ropes."* What's with the rags and worn out clothes? Why did Ebed-melech go to that extra trouble? The Bible doesn't say, but it is safe to use our imagination and assume that Jeremiah's friend wanted to save him the agony of the rope rubbing on his worn down skin and exhausted body. He wanted to soften the strain as they rescued him.

Isn't that such a tender thought? That Jeremiah's friend would *lift him* out of the cistern would be enough, but that he would *lift him gently* and with great care was a visible demonstration of the great love of God for this faithful servant. That's the kind of woman that I want to be. That's how I want my disposition to grow – that I would be an *ezer-lifter*, one who allows my experience of having been lifted out of the pit of misery and despair to lead me to lift others, gently and with great care.

By God's grace, my life with this *ezer* God is producing something profound that He may offer to others who are discouraged, frightened, weary and worn out. Our uniquely feminine disposition flows out of our faith, and having experienced the upholding support of the hand of mighty God for our own lives, we become like Him! Informed by the laments of the prophets, by God's faithfulness throughout the ages to men like Elijah and the sick man at the Bethesda pool, our faith overflows into a disposition to be women who bear the *ezer-lifter* image of God in those sagging places. As the Truth of God's Word and the gracious care of His people lift us, we become more like Him so that we are strong pillars, vertical columns that provide solid support and sustaining care.

The Ecclesiastes 4 Principle

This is not really natural to me. I've already acknowledged my empathy deficit. You can see the connection: No empathy, no lifting. If you don't see the guy in the well, you aren't likely to get out your rope and rags. But I'm growing. As a strategy to live in light of what I want to be, I routinely add the text "Ecclesiastes 4:9,10" to my signature. These words, *"Two are better than one, because they have good reward for their toil. For if they fall, one will lift up his fellow. But woe to him who is alone when he falls and has not another to lift him up!"* are a constant *reminder* of my "old nature" – the one that wants to be left alone – and a *vision* for who I want to be. What if Jeremiah had been alone? Woe to him!

This is my experience of family during this season with my mom. We are entering week fourteen of full-time care, primarily provided by my siblings and me. While I would like to say I have been a "pillar of faith and hope" during these months, that would be sadly untrue. Instead, there are many days that I feel hopeless and tired and discouraged and, frankly, selfish. I have often cried out "How long, Lord? How long?" I have questioned His goodness. I have maligned His plan. I have wanted my life back.

It is on these days, the fallen days, that one of my brothers or sisters…or one of my spiritual siblings…will tuck the rag-covered-rope under my arms and lift me out of the pit. The rope may come in the form of a phone call or text, or a kind email with Scripture promises to remind me of what is true. It may come in the form of tightly closed roses that would open slowly over these days of waiting. It may come, as it has this morning, in the Styrofoam container of beef stew from my favorite diner.

It may come in something as simple as a hug and the silent freedom to weep.

And in the sending down of the rope, I am reminded of what I know is true: God has a plan for my Mom (and for me), to bless her and to prosper her. His purpose will prevail. All things work together for good to those who love God and are called according to His purpose. He loves her with an everlasting love, that He will never leave her nor forsake her, that His ways are higher than our ways.

The Ecclesiastes 4 principle. Russian author Vera Nezarian[113] puts it this way: "Was it you or I who stumbled first? It does not matter. The one of us who finds the strength to get up first must help the other." Two are, indeed, better than one. As God is our *ezer-lifter*, we reflect His image by becoming that for one another. Lifting each other out of despair. Out of fear. Out of disappointment.

In his book *Songs in the Night*, Pastor Mike Milton refers to Brennan Manning's line about singing a "doxology in the darkness." It is rare that we are able to sing such a song in the night on our own. We need one another so that we might manage the dark days with anticipation of God's glory and our good, joining our voices in doxology – a beautifully orchestrated duet, rather than a solo.

Keep On Keeping On

Sometimes the kind of supporting help needed is not so much about *lifting* as it is about *sustaining*. In the 1970s Curtis Mayfield sang "Keep on keeping on," a phrase that became iconic for that generation. I don't know that my dad was a Cur-

113 Vera Nezarian, *The Perpetual Calendar of Inspiration*

tis Mayfield fan, but he borrowed the phrase "keep on keeping on" as a means to encourage us, teaching us to press on, to work hard, to not give up.

Had my dad or Mr. Mayfield been in Virginia Beach in September of 2007, I suspect they would have been sorely disappointed by my first half marathon performance. I had trained for months with a number of friends and we traveled to Virginia Beach over the Labor Day weekend.

The race started early in the morning and by mile 5 (of 13.1), despite my training, I was really struggling. I was not sure I could finish, and I had a long way to go.

I was *really* miserable. About mile 11, I caught a glimpse of several friends who were on the sidelines. They had not come to run, but to cheer. And they were cheering! They yelled encouragement and took pictures and high-fived me. But I was fading. Fast. "Keep on keeping on"? I don't think so.

One of my friends knew I wasn't looking too confident. Without hesitation, she came off the sidelines and started running with me. She did not have on running shoes. She was not a runner. But she stayed with me and talked to me and pushed me and encouraged me.

With the finish line in view, she put her hand on my back and literally pushed me through that last quarter-mile to the finish line. I would not have gotten there without her.

Keep on keeping on.

This is the kind of sustaining help that Moses received from Aaron and Hur during the battle against the Amalekites described in Exodus 17. "*Whenever Moses held up his hand, Israel prevailed, and whenever he lowered his hand, Amalek prevailed. But Moses' hands grew weary, so they took a stone and put it under him, and he sat on it, while Aaron and Hur held up his hands, one on one side, and the other on the other side.* **So his hands were steady until the going down of the sun.**" Moses was unable to sustain the strength needed to carry on. And so the Lord gave him Aaron and Hur.

I was unable to get to the finish line. And so the Lord gave me Jill.

Sometimes we just need someone to be "in it" with us, to stay the course, to remind us to "keep on keeping on." I suspect this is why Jesus sent His disciples out in pairs,[114] and why Paul always traveled with a ministry partner. Life is hard. We lose our perspective and we grow weary. We lose sight of the goal. We want, with every fiber of our being, to quit. And so the Lord sends Aaron, or Hur, or Jill.

This is the disposition of the *ezer*-helper. Having experienced the sustaining grace of my Heavenly Father, I want very much to become that kind of woman. The one who holds up the left arm of a weary leader while another holds up his right. The one who puts my hand on the back of a worn-out friend and pushes her through to the finish line of a worthy goal. The one who travels *with* people, helping them to "keep on keeping on."

This is not moralistic support. It is not a patronizing, let-me-do-you-a-favor kind of help. It is, rather, a work of the Holy Spirit in us and for others. It is the *ezer-lifter* God coming to us in the comfort and care of one another. It is what it means to bear the *helper* image of God.

Rehab Addict Indeed

We live in a culture that is not kind. We are, each of us to a different degree, beaten and weathered by the harsh elements of

114 Luke 10:1

the day. Our house is sagging. But God, who is our strong support, the upholder of our very lives, is not far off. It is the Gospel that provides the vertical post that protects us from lateral disintegration. We will not fall down, not because of our own effort; on the contrary, we – like the invalid by the Bethesda pool – are helpless on our own. Instead, we cling to the truth that the Eternal God is Himself our support. He has lifted us from the "valley of the shadow of death" by the sacrifice of His Son. The Gospel reminds us that the Man of Sorrows is the New Man. The Resurrected, *lifted* Man. He will sustain us by His Work and Word every moment of every day until He comes again to take us home.

In the meantime, such faith informs and inflames my *ezer* image-bearing. This is the theology of the "L" in my helper disposition and it is the natural response to my growing capacity for *empathy*. I long to become a woman who *empathizes* with those who are weary and disappointed and discouraged and afraid, engaging with them through the Gospel to put those padded ropes under their arms and lift them from the muddy pit. I want my faith to overflow so that I am able to come alongside my weary friend to help her finish her race! This is my creation design.

Such lifting and sustaining is not always easy – or even welcome. Sometimes the rope that is needed to pull a weary friend out of the muddy cistern is Truth that is painful and costly. I cannot *always* offer a way out that is comfortable or warm because occasionally the Truth requires difficult choices and heartbreaking repentance. Certainly this was the pattern of Jesus with His friends. He regularly rescued them, lifting them from their own destruction ... but very often such lifting *felt* harsh.

But oh what a difference *ezer*-image-bearing women will make for the Kingdom. As we make it our practice to *lift* people out of despair and *sustain* them on their journey with Christ, we may participate with Him in restoring sadly neglected lives, sagging from despair. As our own lives are changed, we become, as the psalmist described, "*daughters like corner pillars cut for the structure of a palace.*"[115]

Pillars in the palace. Now **that**'s a rehab project worth investing in!

IMPORTANT NOTE: This chapter is not meant to address issues related to severe depression. While I believe that the Scriptures adequately and fully address such serious, life-altering challenges, we must differentiate problems that are physical from those that are spiritual. Typically, as with all of life, there is a connection between the two. However, physical problems ought not be dismissed and should be referred to a medical doctor.

115 Psalm 144:12

Chapter Seven

A CINDERELLA STORY

"P" is for Promoter

In the spring of 1758 the widow Martha Custis welcomed a visitor to her home who intended to court her. His name was George Washington and he had already earned a reputation in the military for fairness, bravery and immense personal courage. George found Martha charming and attractive, and they were married early in 1759.

The onset of the American Revolution permanently changed the course of Martha's life. In 1775, when George was named Commander-in-Chief of the newly formed professional army, Martha immediately became a public figure. She did not relish her new notoriety. Martha was personally very private, preferring the comfort of her own home and family to the company of dignitaries, war heroes and government officials. Even so, she was George's partner in every aspect of their lives.

Throughout the war, Martha traveled from their home in Mt. Vernon to be with her husband on the battlefield during the winter months. During these seasons when the fighting was at a standstill, the General could be aloof and had a bad temper. He was given to self-doubt and melancholy. Martha was his sounding board and closest confidante. Her presence had a calming and positive effect on him. She served as his secretary and representative, copying his correspondence and attending official functions in his stead. She acted as hostess to political leaders, dignitaries, and military officials so that – even on the battlefield – Washington's headquarters were warm, welcoming and generous. One account suggests that "extraordinary Martha was the General's source of strength during the war's most critical hours."[116]

At the end of the war, Martha hoped to return to the relative quiet of a domestic, peaceful private life with her husband, children and grandchildren. In May, 1789, however, George was elected to be the first president under the new U.S. Constitution. Martha followed him bravely to New York City, the temporary capital for the new national government. Here, as on the battlefield, she set aside her own longing for privacy, seeking instead to advance the reputation of her husband as she welcomed visitors, made social calls on important members of society and hosted a weekly reception, held on Friday evenings for anyone who would like to attend. Her warm hospitality made her husband, who continued to be typically reserved, feel at ease and her guests feel welcome.

Martha Washington, the worthy partner of the worthiest of men,[117] was a pivotal factor in George Washington's effective leadership of this very young country. One writer has said: "A close inspection reveals Martha's fingerprints all over George Washington's public life. So much so that it is not unreasonable to suggest that, without Martha, George would never have been president."

The faith-filled disposition of a *helper*, designed by God and made in His own *ezer* image, demonstrates itself in her desire to **P**romote the plans and purposes of God in the lives of His people. She seeks to cultivate and tend a **H**edge of protection; she **E**mpathizes and **L**ifts others. But she does not stop there. As Martha did for George, the *ezer* recognizes the great, good

116 www.whitehouse.gov
117 www.marthawashington.us/Alexandria Advertiser & Commercial Intelligencer, May 25, 1802

purpose of God and determines to promote His purpose in His people. This aspect of her *ezer* design, like the others, is informed by Scripture and rooted in her faith. She has experienced this *ezer* nature of God in her own life and she is eager for such a disposition that overflows into the lives of others.

Puppies and Clydesdales

We typically think of the idea of "promotion" in the context of the professional world, which is appropriate. A promotion, for an aspiring young professional, typically means more responsibility and more money. The budding seed of the American Dream. We also think of "promotion" in terms of a product and its advertising campaign. Prior to watching a recent commercial, I would not have known that the silent story of a friendship between a Clydesdale and a puppy might sell me a beer. However, the latest television ad for Budweiser is so heartwarming that even the most committed teetotaler might be tempted to buy a six-pack. Genius.

The dictionary defines the word *promote* with each of these nuances. However, as I think about biblical womanhood, particularly around the *ezer* image of God, this is the definition that describes her disposition to **P**romote the plans and purposes of God: "to encourage the growth or development of something or someone."[118] Synonyms include words like "advance," "advocate," "endorse," stimulate," "improve," "push" ... you get the idea.

But how does such thinking resonate with our theology – what we know to be true about God? Or does it?

A Cinderella Story

"Of old you spoke in a vision to your godly one, and said: 'I have

118 Bing dictionary

granted ezer to one who is mighty; I have exalted one chosen from the people. I have found David, my servant; with my holy oil I have anointed him."

These verses are found in Psalm 89, a psalm that practically bellows the confidence of its author in his covenant-keeping God. Beginning here and continuing for more than twenty verses, he recounts the faithfulness of God to keep His promises, particularly as they relate to David's kingdom and the ultimate outcome of his reign. Over and over, Ethan recounts the words of the Lord about His own purposes and plans: "I will" (nine times!), "my hand," "my faithfulness," "my love." The psalmist, and all of Israel with him, recognized and celebrated David's kingship as a special gift of God's love to His people.

Note especially in the verses above the attention given to God's *ezer* help. *"I have granted ezer."* How? *"I have exalted one chosen from the people."* In case we've forgotten, the psalmist takes this opportunity to remind the people "from whence he [the King!] has come." This could be the original "Cinderella story," the king who was born the last of eight sons. The runt. The kid who was almost forgotten by his father as he presented the older, better-looking, more skilled and more prepared brothers to the prophet Samuel as he looked for Israel's next king. Like Cinderella excluded from the ball, David was left in the fields by his father and brothers, not invited to the anointing ceremony because surely he did not have what it would take to be king.

But God had not lost sight of the boy in the fields. True, David, of all the boys, was the least prepared, the least experienced, and the least likely to succeed. Yet in God's economy, none of these were barriers to the throne. David's crown was unlikely, but God's plan had been in play from the beginning and it would not be spoiled.

The story of David's kingship begins in 1 Samuel 16. Israel's first king, Saul, had turned from God and threatened to lead the nation of Israel away from Jehovah. So God set about recruiting Saul's replacement by sending his servant, Samuel, to the house of a man named Jesse. Here, the Lord told Samuel, *"I have provided for myself a king among his [Jesse's] sons."*

The next few verses tell the story of Jesse parading each of his sons before Samuel (are you picturing Anastasia and Drusilla preening before the Handsome Prince?) as the Lord whispers in the prophet's ear, "No, not this one." After the seventh son had come forward for inspection by Samuel and been subsequently rejected, Samuel asked Jesse, "Is this it? Are there others?" (loose translation). *"There remains the youngest, but behold he is keeping the sheep."*[119] In other words, "Yes. There is another. But he is so insignificant that he isn't worth mentioning, and certainly not worth your time."

David was the youngest and the smallest. While the three oldest brothers had already proven themselves in battle alongside Saul,[120] little brother David composed music in the fields as he wandered the hillside with the sheep. But the brothers did not impress the Lord, and Jesse's opinion did not sway Samuel from his duty. *"Arise,"* the Scripture records God speaking to Samuel as David approaches from the fields, *"anoint him, for this is he."*[121] The glass slipper on the foot of Cinderella.

Psalm 78:70 records that the Lord *"... chose David, his servant, and took him from the sheepfolds; from following the nursing ewes he brought him to shepherd Jacob his people, Israel his inheritance."* Did you catch that? He chose David. Some years later, when David needed a reminder, God would send Nathan the prophet to him

119 1 Samuel 16:11
120 1 Samuel 17:13
121 1 Samuel 16:12

and this is what Nathan said: *"Thus says the Lord of Hosts, 'I took you from the pasture, from following the sheep, that you should be Prince over my people Israel."* [122]

He chose David. He took the shepherd from the pasture and made him the prince.

I love this series of events that the Sovereign Lord orchestrated so that he could demonstrate His own character and nature. It was not David's power and prowess that would make him a great king. He had virtually nothing to offer. Yet God *promoted* the young shepherd boy from the nursing of the ewes to the throne of a great kingdom because this was what David was created for. It was God's plan for David to spend himself on behalf of the people, to lead them with skill and affection and great devotion for the Lord.

David never lost sight of the unlikelihood of his crown. He would have known that he was the least-likely-to-be-named-king. His lineage was respectable, but not illustrious. His family was godly, but not noticeably so. And he, of all the boys, was the least prepared or experienced for this highest calling in the land.

But God's redemptive plan for all of history included this young man's promotion to the throne. Ultimately, the Messiah would come from the line of David. It was in the city of David that the Baby Jesus would be born. The covenant that God made with David would be a turning point in the outworking of His saving purposes, *"And your house and your kingdom shall be made sure forever before me. Your Throne shall be established forever."* [123] God had a plan and a purpose for the shepherd-who-would-be-king. So God promoted him.

122 2 Samuel 7:8
123 2 Samuel 7:16

The Thread of Helper-Promoter Theology

This theology of God our helper who promotes His people according to His own plans and purposes resonates throughout all of Scripture. David seems an obvious example. But what about Moses, and Gideon, and Daniel? How about Samuel himself? He was just a boy when he first heard the voice of the Lord calling to him in the temple. The Old Testament narrative of the redemptive nature of God recounts one circumstance after another of Jehovah God granting *ezer*, exalting "regular guys" to positions of great influence and power. He provides for Himself a prophet. A commander-in-chief. A priest. A pharaoh (Joseph!). Over and over He *chooses one from among the people* to accomplish His purposes and plans and He, alone, makes the promotion.

The God of the New Covenant grants *ezer* in no less dramatic fashion. Consider Peter. You may know that his name was not always "Peter." Matthew records the name-change in chapter 16: *"And I tell you, you are Peter, and on this rock I will build my church, and the gates of hell shall not prevail against it."* His name was originally *Simon* Peter, but Jesus changed his name to "Rock" (Peter), serving as a reminder of this great vision for Peter's life and ministry: "*On this rock I will build my church.*" That's pretty impressive. Jesus would build His church on the rock of Peter's ministry.

But Peter's life was not always so impressive. Just a cursory glance at Peter's résumé makes Jesus' confidence in him more astounding.

Peter. The one who walked on the water ... and then sank.[124]

Peter. The one who "*rebuked* Jesus"![125]

124 Matthew 14:29
125 Matthew 16:22

Peter. The one who wanted to build the tents for Moses, Elijah and Jesus.[126]

Peter. The one who fell asleep in the garden while Jesus prayed.[127]

Peter. The one who cut off the guard's ear in the garden.[128]

Peter. The one who denied Jesus *three times.*[129]

Peter. Bless his heart. (That's what we say in the South about people who have obviously come up short in some way. It's Southern charm for: "What an idiot.") Peter, on his own, was a boorish, ill-mannered, quick-tongued fisherman. He was rough and loud. He was uneducated. And, by all accounts, he failed Jesus on more than one occasion.

But the Savior saw something different. After commending Peter for his clear confession of faith, Jesus would promote Peter from buffoon to *foundation stone of the church*.

It was the practice of the Savior to call people out of their less-than-impressive lives into something much more dramatic, much more hope-filled, much more eternal. He promoted fishermen to preachers. Persecutors to apostles. Prostitutes to evangelists. For His own purpose and to advance His own plan, Jesus deployed uneducated ruffians and *women* (in the eastern world these were *less than* ruffians). But, as we've seen in part, this was not a new strategy.

Man of Sorrows

Generations before Jesus would call Peter as the foundation stone of the church, Isaiah would describe the Messiah in his well-rehearsed prophecy:

126 Matthew 17:1
127 Matthew 26:40
128 John 18:10
129 Luke 22:60, 61

"...he had no form or majesty that we should look at him,
and no beauty that we should desire him.
He was despised and rejected by men;
a man of sorrows, and acquainted with grief;
and as one from whom men hide their faces he was despised,
and we esteemed him not."[130]

If I didn't know better, I would think I was reading a description of the Hunchback of Notre Dame. Or Attila the Hun. Or the Wicked Witch of the West.

But these verses are not from a fairy tale. They are the prophetic utterance of Isaiah as he looks on the horizon of mankind and sees the deliverance of God. Oddly, it is not a great warrior riding on a white horse who would rescue us from our sin. Instead, our salvation would come in the form of a poor carpenter who had no discernible king-like qualities. The popular crowd of His time and even His own family would reject Him.

And yet, when we look once more at the Apostle Paul's letter to the Philippians, we read these words (again!) about the carpenter-king:

"Though He was in the form of God, He did not consider equality with God a thing to be grasped [held onto], but made himself nothing, taking the form of a servant and being born in the likeness of man. And being found in human form, He humbled Himself by becoming obedient to the point of death, even death on a cross. Therefore God has exalted Him and bestowed on Him the name that is above every name, so that at the name of Jesus, every knee should bow in heaven and on earth and under the earth and every tongue should confess that Jesus Christ is Lord to the glory of God the Father."[131]

God has exalted Him. This is the ultimate picture of God's

130 Isaiah 53:2-3
131 Philippians 2:6-11

ezer-promotion. Looking back to Psalm 89, Ethan's recounting of God's covenant-keeping promotion of David, Charles Spurgeon instructs that this psalm is ultimately about God's relationship to Christ. Spurgeon identifies Christ, by His birth, as "one of the people" ... just a regular guy by virtue of His parents, His birthplace, and His education. To the untrained eye, He was – much like David – a nobody. And yet, He was elected, chosen by God, to satisfy His justice and restore our kinship with Him. Finally, as Paul has so beautifully recorded in Philippians: out of His obedience, Jesus was exalted above all of the elect. Promoted, in the most powerful and holy form of the word, so that now He sits at the right hand of God the Father Almighty.

"I have exalted one chosen from the people." Doesn't that make you want to exclaim: HALLELUJAH!

This is the theology that informs our ability to grow in our *ezer* helper disposition. God routinely grants *ezer* by promoting His people to accomplish His own plans and purposes. Both our *knowledge* of this aspect of God's nature and our *experience* of it inform and inflame our desire to be His image-bearers.

Looking Out for Number One

It does not take long, however, to discover how shallow is our desire to be this kind of *ezer* helper. A good friend who served on staff with me for a time pointed this out for me after one of our staff meetings. It was my habit, during these meetings, to ask my coworkers how I could pray for them. After sharing about my own needs, we routinely went around the circle to give each person the opportunity to talk for a bit about what was happening in her life and how we could pray. This particular day as I met one-on-one with Tracy following our staff meeting, she asked, "You do care about what's going on in their lives, don't you?" "Of course I do," I replied with some indignation. "Do you realize that, after you have talked about yourself and your own family, there is very little time left for everyone else to share?" she suggested gently. Uh ... no. I hadn't realized that. Once I recovered from my justified humiliation, I knew she was right. I typically spent so much time talking about myself that I monopolized what little time we had. It was a habit that was not limited to that particular gathering. Over the course of the next months, I realized that I do that *a lot*. At the expense of everyone else in the room, I hear myself talking about my family or myself. To this day, I have to say to myself: "Do not tell that story. No one needs to hear that. Let someone else talk."

Sigh.

What happened in that staff meeting illustrates what goes on in my heart (even if unintentionally) when I am at my worst. I want to be noticed. I want to be funny. I want to be the best. I want to be the winner.

Notice that *I* am the common denominator. Self-promoting. Self-preserving. Self-serving. Singer Travis Tritt affirms the bent of my selfish soul:

> "Lord everyone around me
>
> I've tried so hard to please
>
> Til the only one unhappy
>
> Feeling broken down is me
>
> But things are gonna change
>
> With each new setting sun
>
> Starting now, I'm looking out for Number One."

Looking out for number one. I am the only person I need to please. Not exactly a paragon of *ezer* virtue, eh?

Selfies and Other Weird Stuff

Travis and I are not alone. This notion of self-ism, looking out for Number One, has become a generational value. To be self-aware, self-possessing, self-confident, and self-preserving is an art form that has been perfected by our peers. The advent of social media has fueled the flame of "self" as we update our Facebook® status throughout the day, assuming that people care that we are "on the road to NY" or "cooking pancakes for dinner" or "out on a date with my amazing hubby." And people feed our self-focused appetite because they "like" and/or "comment" on our status with some regularity. We Tweet and Snapchat® and Instagram® every detail of our lives as if each particular activity or thought or feeling is monumental. Blogging is the new graffiti since the web is free and available to anyone who can type. And every post, every status update, every tweet & Instagram® is about *me*, *myself* and *I* (or *my* children, *my* husband, *my* dog).

The most glaring illustration of the self-consumed psyche of our generation is the aptly named "selfie." This trend is almost creepy. I am regularly amazed by the phenomenon of people taking pictures of themselves *and posting them* for all the world to see. Admittedly, one reason I think it's crazy is because I've actually taken a picture of myself – and it's not attractive. I just can't figure out how to get the camera angled so that I don't look like I have a double chin and sagging eyelids. But even if I *could* take a picture of myself that was decent, I can't imagine "posting" it. That just seems so…well, self-absorbed.

And we're back to where we began.

The Voice of the New Woman

Susan Hunt, author of *The True Woman*, indicted an earlier generation of women but her characterization is sadly prophetic of this age as a whole: "We have absorbed an egocentric worldview into our souls without realizing it ... the voice of the new woman is unrestrained, immature self-ism." This idea of "me, myself and I" is becoming so instinctive that it is pervasive. We are being self-absorbed, promoting our own self-interest, even when we don't know it.

I recently read an article in *Forbes* magazine titled "The One Thing Female Leaders Should be Doing More Of."[132] The focus of the article is that women leaders should be mentoring younger women. A suggestion that seems very altruistic and others-oriented. Then the entire article goes on to describe the *mentor's* benefits from mentoring.

> Stress relief.
>
> Build resilience.
>
> Remind you of how accomplished you are.
>
> Give you a chance to learn, too.
>
> Develop your sense of purpose.

Why should you mentor younger women? Because it's good for *you*. Now, I suspect that the author of this article would heartily agree that the *main* reason you should become a mentor is because it is good for the younger woman, but it is just an interesting selling point that there's something in it for the mentor. Instead of mentoring being a means of selfless service on behalf of someone else, something that one might do for no reason other than to give back, it becomes a means to the mentor's own gain. Relieving stress. Getting stronger. Feeling prideful. Gaining insight and wisdom. Being purposeful. Nuanced

132 *Forbes Magazine*, www.forbes.com, January 21, 2014

self-ism. Egoism disguised as altruism.

Then there's the other side of the coin described in Lois Frankel's book *Nice Girls Don't Get the Corner Office*. Here, the author explains the value of office politics as a means to get things done.

"A successful workplace relationship, whether with a boss or a co-worker, is one in which you clearly define what you have to offer and what you need or want from the other person. It happens all the time without putting a name to it ... the trade is implicit in the relationship ... Each time you go out of your way for someone or give them what they need, you've earned a figurative 'chip' that you can later cash in for something *you* need."[133]

I recognize the challenge to succeed for a woman in the workplace, but the suggestion that her relationships are a means to her personal advancement, an economic venture that is measured by the number of "chips" collected borders on being offensive. Even for this generation.

In a devotional titled "Women: The Road Ahead", Elisabeth Elliot quoted a then-current leading news magazine: "There's not a woman anywhere who made it in business who is not tough, self-centered, and enormously aggressive."[134]

If this is the voice of the new woman, I think I'd like to go back to the old one, please.

The need to self-protect and self-promote may present itself in something as harmless as my personal storytelling during our staff meeting. But the competitive nature of our culture stirs in us the need to ensure our own advancement at any cost. This is why people cheat on tests, lie on job applications, embezzle funds, and steal ideas.

133 *Nice Girls Don't Get the Corner Office*, Lois P. Frankel, p. 38
134 *Keep a Quiet Heart*, Elisabeth Elliot, p. 213

The lengths to which we will go to promote ourselves. Unrestrained self-ism indeed.

A Deep Desire to Have My Own Way. Even at Church.

The church is not exempt. Both Paul and James speak to the danger of selfish ambition, and both men were writing to Christians.[135] The *ESV Study Bible* defines "selfish ambition" as "a divisive willingness to split the group in order to achieve personal power and prestige." My version: "a deep desire to have your own way even at the expense of others."

Our experience of this in the church has many facets. We see "selfish ambition" when people complain about the music, or the sermon, or the youth ministry, or the children's ministry, or the women's ministry. No matter what the arena, this is the common objection: "They just don't meet my needs." There are many forms of this grievance:

"I don't feel moved by the Spirit when I'm there,"

"The sermon is too long,"

"There is too much emphasis on the Bible" (Yes. I've actually heard this one),

"There's not enough emphasis on the Bible,"

"They don't embrace my children,"

"They don't meet at a convenient time" and on and on.

In some cases some of these complaints may be valid. But I would suggest that, in general, if you peel away all the layers of fluff and niceties, at the core of each of these grumblings is SELF. Me. Myself. I. My preferences. My schedule. My needs. Me.

135 Philippians 2 and James 3

When I was in Children's Ministries, we had a season during which it was particularly difficult to recruit volunteers. I use the word "season" loosely. Difficult recruiting season was pretty much year round. So we came up with a plan to require members to serve in the nursery for one hour each month.

Let me be clear: one hour. Each month. That's one hour out of seven hundred and twenty (for the thirty-day months). Or, if you just assume the *church* hours, it's one hour out of eighteen, give or take thirty minutes.

That idea almost cost me my job. People *left the church* because they did not want to be "forced" to serve in the nursery. They left. The Church. **Selfish ambition.**

I can almost see you nodding your head in disdain. If that's you in my mind's eye, I just want you to ask yourself: "If the elders and staff of my church told me that – after careful deliberation, prayer and strategizing – they needed me to serve in the nursery for one hour every month for the whole year, *would I do it? Cheerfully*?"

A Faith-Filled Disposition

Don't give up. Even as I write this chapter, I am tempted to be incredibly discouraged – by the self-preserving bent of my own nature and by what I see as I consider the cultural landscape. It seems that we are becoming more myopic by the decade.

But the words of Paul in 2 Corinthians rescue me from my despair: *"But we have this treasure in jars of clay to show that the surpassing power belongs to God and not to us. So we are afflicted in every way, but not crushed; perplexed, but not driven to despair; persecuted but not forsaken; struck down, but not destroyed ... for we are always being given over to death for Jesus' sake, so that the life of*

Jesus may also be manifested in our mortal flesh ... We do not lose heart."[136] Sisters, our uniquely feminine disposition flows out of our faith. Our ability to become women who are driven not by selfish ambition but by a deep desire to see the will of God come to pass in the lives of others is directly related to "the life of Jesus being manifested in our mortal flesh." Informed by Psalm 89 and the heritage found in David's rise to royalty as well as New Covenant testimony such as Peter's and Paul's, we grow in our faith. Christ, having been rejected by men but *exalted* by God because of His obedience, gives us the power and passion to give our self-promoting nature "over to death." Finally, we may look forward to becoming women who bear the *ezer promoter* image of God.

The Truth Hurts

Over the past decade or so there has been a television show dedicated to discovering amateur musicians who then compete for the opportunity to win a recording contract. I do not watch every episode every season and in fact, the past few seasons I have not watched much at all. The auditions, however, are particularly entertaining – in a "this-is-a-train-wreck-but-I-can't-look-away" fashion. It is amazing to me that people come to an audition, boldly stand before three judges who have made a career out of the music business . . . and absolutely butcher a song. I'm no virtuoso, but I know "on key" when I hear it, and I'm absolutely stunned by the *really bad* "singers" who hope to get the golden ticket.

What's particularly odd, and sad, is the Mom, Dad, Grandmother, Aunt, Uncle or other random family member who has told that child for years that she can sing! "Baby, you can do anything you put your mind to! You are a great singer. If you

136 2 Corinthians 4:7-10, 16

want to be the next American singing sensation, you just have to work hard and *go for it*! You can do it."

Actually, no. You can't do it. Those young people stand in front of the judges and sing their tone-deaf hearts out, only to finally hear the truth: "Sweetheart, this ain't for you." Their dreams are dashed by strangers and many leave the audition in tears. Those starstruck hopefuls, empowered by the words of their well-meaning relatives, run head-long into the truth and are shocked by its resonance. Sometimes, the damage done by unsubstantiated affirmation is deep and recovery is difficult.

Engaging in the promotion of others as an *ezer* does not mean standing behind them, unequivocally assuring them: "You can do anything! You can be anything you want to be! The world is your oyster!" I have heard well-meaning Christians deploy Philippians 4:13 in this manner. They hope to affirm and empower by their use of the Word. But, number one, it is not true that you can be anything that you want to be and, number two, that is not what Paul meant. The words *"I can do all things through Christ who strengthens me"* are not a call to leap tall buildings in a single bound…they are, instead, a call to live in whatever circumstances God has ordained for you – wealthy, poor, imprisoned, sick, healthy…these are the "all things" that Paul refers to. It is these things that Christ strengthens us for. In no way is the Apostle suggesting that Jesus will give us the strength (and/or ability) to do whatever we want to do.

This season, one of the current judges on the aforementioned show recently remarked: "The best thing we can do for these kids is to tell them the truth. Every one of them has something special – but it might not be music, and someone needs to tell them so."[137] As my dad used to say, "the truth hurts."

137 Loosely quoted from Keith Urban on American Idol

Our *ezer* disposition helps people to discover the unique and particular gifts that God has given them. We watch them succeed and fail, and we give them real perspective about where they might excel and be effective. We are honest with them about their shortcomings (we all have them!) and we challenge them to grow in the areas where they are obviously gifted. We offer our own experience or we lead them to others who can so that they will learn, improve, and succeed in accomplishing the purpose and plan of God for their lives.

The Story of a College Dropout

Several years ago I decided to audit a course at the seminary in our city. It had been more than twenty-five years since I had been in a classroom, so I was a little nervous. As I arrived early and found an empty seat in the room full of very young – mostly male – students, the proverbial "fish out of water" ran through my mind. Literally every other person in the room had a "tablet" or a laptop and, as they scrambled to set up their space, I realized how old I really am. I sheepishly pulled out my pristine legal pad and my Pilot pen pack and hoped no one would notice me.

That prospect was dashed as the professor welcomed the 50+ students by going around the room asking each of us to introduce ourselves and tell where we graduated from college, just as a means to get to know one another. I had to fight a rising panic as the sharing exercise made its way to the last row, where I had taken a seat. I hate the "where did you graduate" question. It makes me feel very unaccomplished and inadequate because I dropped out of college after a couple of years. It's a long story.

I married young, had two children and was primarily their mom and Chas' wife at the time when most people today are finishing college and doing graduate work. My entrée into ministry came because my mother was instrumental in launching a Bible Study Fellowship effort in our town and she needed a children's leader. I had no experience and no qualifications. But those years in BSF were a strategic training ground for me, and my participation on that leadership team ignited a spark of affection for ministry that has continued to grow for almost thirty years.

During my years in children's ministry, I was given the opportunity and freedom to think outside the box, to be creative and to take risks. One of our pastoral staff met regularly with me and he both challenged and affirmed my efforts. He encouraged me to attend workshops and seminars so that I would gain knowledge from folks who had experience. His leadership was a great gift to me during those years.

As I made the transition to women's ministry, another of our pastors became my supervisor and cheerleader. He helped me to hone my teaching skills by working with me on notes and outlines. He read and critiqued Bible study curriculum that I developed. He gently refined my shepherding ability by discussing issues and challenges that women were facing.

I have a team of women who serve with me as leaders, without whom I would be lost. They meet with me several times a month to help me to think critically and strategically. They keep me focused. They are honest with me both about my own shortcomings and about the areas of ministry that need to be refined.

I am a college dropout. Whatever effective ministry I have enjoyed has been because of the faithfulness of God to allow for the *promoting* efforts of His people on my behalf. In his book *A Song in the Night*, pastor Mike Milton credits Michelangelo, who saw David in that great stone slab when others saw only a rock.[138] I love that illustration. It resonates with Paul's words to the Ephesians from chapter 2, *"For we are His workmanship,"* the word translated there means literally "work of art." Each person who is part of my history has chipped away at the stone, carving away the excess so that the work of art would be exposed.

I want so much to be *that kind of woman.* Our *ezer* disposition overflows as we are willing to sacrifice, to spend ourselves in an effort to *promote* others so that they are able to accomplish the great, good purpose of God for their lives. We gladly invest time, effort, space, emotional energy, and sometimes money to help reveal the work of art that God has planned. Such *ezer* is not always glamorous or immediately obviously successful, but the outcome of the story belongs to the Lord. Who knows what that chisel will uncover?

It Comes Down to This

Ours is a world that celebrates self. Magazine covers, music, advertising campaigns, book titles and blog stories encourage us to make ourselves happy, ensure our own success and protect our own comfort. We are encouraged to improve our self-esteem by praising ourselves, speaking up for ourselves, being proud of ourselves, accepting ourselves. Admittedly, the competition to "get ahead" is fierce, and it is tempting to do whatever is necessary to reserve our piece of the pie.

But God is faithful. His covenant-keeping commitment echoes through the ages as we remember David, the shepherd-king ... and Moses, and Gideon, Daniel, Peter, and Paul. The New Covenant reveals the ultimate *ezer* act of promotion as the sum of prophetic history finds its fulfillment in the exaltation of Christ. The desperate need to promote ourselves is lost

138 Mike Milton, *A Song in the Night*, p. 76

as we trust the Faithful One.

I am regularly stunned by His *ezer* promotion in my life. I, much like David, bring very little of value to the table. And as you've read my story throughout these past several chapters, you see that my past is riddled with failure and sin. I am deeply aware of the condition of my soul absent the Gospel. Who am I that God would allow me to serve Him in any capacity, let alone in ministry? This is Christ in me, the display of God's redemptive grace. Full of gratitude, I am a walking testimony to His *ezer* promoting nature.

This is the faith that informs and inflames our *ezer* image-bearing. This is the theology of the last letter of our HELP acrostic. Our *promoter* disposition flows out of our faith and we find ourselves growing in our capacity to help others find and succeed in the good purpose of God for their lives.

However, as with each of the former aspects of our unique womanhood, this *promoting* disposition will not come without a cost. Martha Washington's *promotion* of her husband's effective leadership, both as a General and as our inaugural President, required that, to some degree, she leave "self" behind. She was by George's side, when she would have preferred to be with her children and grandchildren. She entertained prominent guests, when she might have preferred a quiet cup of tea and a book of verse. She moved to the city, when she preferred the peaceful surrounding of land and countryside.

This is the *ezer* image-bearing life. Is it costly? It is. But the return on the investment is eternal. Hear the words of Jesus, the ultimate *ezer*: "*For whoever would save his life will lose it, but whoever loses his life for my sake will find it.*"[139] Amen?

139 Matthew 19:25

Chapter Eight

A PUZZLE OF IMMENSE PROPORTION

H.E.L.P. A very simple, but not-so-easy acrostic that serves as a framework for thinking biblically about womanhood. Our E.Z.E.R. image-bearing cannot be fully captured in this four-letter mnemonic, but it is at least a beginning.

Since our children have been gone, I have taken up jigsaw puzzles. I know it's old-fashioned and not very flashy, but there is something immensely satisfying in sorting the pieces into straight-edges and corners, colors, patterns and scenes. I love to watch the picture come together so that what begins as a thousand random pieces that do not appear to belong together at all becomes the beautiful scene displayed on the box top. Whether I am working on a black-and-white scene from the New York harbor or a Technicolor® display of dozens of cupcakes, I am amazed every time at the order and beauty of the pieces rightly arranged and fit together.

Although everyone has a different approach, there is a certain strategy to this craft. Most puzzlers begin by turning over all the pieces, looking for those pieces that are part of the "frame," the straight edges. Once this is done, I have a habit of setting out plastic tumblers and as I sort the puzzle into sections, each tumbler is filled with pieces that seem to belong together.

Now the actual construction of the puzzle can begin. The four corners are placed generally where it seems they should belong, and the straight edges are set and connected to form the frame of the puzzle. The inside really only begins to make sense once this border is complete.

If we think about the theology of biblical womanhood as a beautiful puzzle, each letter from the four-letter acrostic may serve as one of the corners. The straight edges are made up of all of the Scripture that we have studied and each of the lives of God's people that has informed our thinking. Now we have a frame, a border for an exquisite picture. The tumblers are lined up and we can begin to work on the inside, section by section.

You may already be dumping out those plastic tumblers, anxiously setting the pieces upright so that you can begin to plug them into the picture. You have set that frame into place with each of the corners and all of the edges secure and you are ready to keep going. Your enthusiasm is commendable.

Or, you may be at the other end of the jigsaw puzzle experience. We have covered so much material and the border alone terrifies you. Just getting those straight-edges together may have been exhausting and you just aren't sure you have it in you to sift through every tumbler to complete the picture. Maybe this puzzle seems like too much and you are tempted to toss all the pieces back in the box. Your reluctance is understandable.

At this point, we *have* covered a lot of ground. As I have had this conversation in coffee shops and conferences, I've discovered that much of what we've learned here is new for many women. Even those who have been reared in Christian homes with faithful and godly moms have felt overwhelmed and a little apprehensive as they have taken in these truths and thoughtfully considered how they apply to their walk with God and their relationships with others. So if you are terrified by the tumblers full of puzzle pieces, take a deep breath. You are in good company!

Hope for the Overwhelmed

Recently, I had occasion to teach for several weeks on the topic of "*What it means to be uniquely feminine in the body of Christ.*" Each Wednesday evening, as women came into the classroom from dinner, one bright, enthusiastic newlywed made her way to the front row. She listened, took notes and engaged in the discussion as we worked through much of this material. When I gave the women a bibliography of helpful books on the subject of godly womanhood, she promptly went to the library and checked out every title that was available (there were more than twelve!). As she and I began a friendship and continued a personal dialog on God's design for women, I received an email from her. Here's an excerpt:

"You see, I love my husband but I don't love domesticity. I'm a horrible cook and I do not iron. I'm fairly certain that I could be a good cook, but I get horribly distracted by books. Last week I made this atrocious chicken dish. I felt so bad. It tasted horrible. The next night I fetched fast food. But most of the time I do OK, just not fancy. Mostly I've been concentrating really hard on 'loving' ... on trying to make sure that our home is a peaceful, accepting place for Michael[140] to be. Which is much harder than it looks on paper, because I work full time and have a 45 minute commute and then I cook and then I clean. (Because even when the dinner tastes horrible, you still have a sink full of dishes.) But I've been working on doing it all without (too much) griping."

Reading Jenny's email made me smile. She certainly got an "A" for effort, but you don't have to read between the lines to see that she was overwhelmed by "doing it all". I looked forward to our next conversation for several reasons, but at the

140 Not their real names

very least, I wanted Jenny to realize that putting the puzzle of biblical womanhood together takes time. Lots of time. It cannot be assembled in an evening, or a week, or even a month. It's called "transformation" and it takes a lifetime.

Paul remarks on this expectation in his second letter to the church at Corinth.

"And we all, with unveiled face, beholding the glory of the Lord, are ***being transformed into the same image*** *from one degree of glory to another. For this comes from the Lord who is the Spirit."*[141]

Notice that Paul talks about *being transformed* into the image of Jesus. He does not say we *are* transformed, or that we *have been transformed.* He says that we are *being transformed.* This becoming more and more like the woman that God designed at the time of creation, the one made in His image, is a process. It takes place over time and is not instantaneous.

It is also significant that Paul reminds the Corinthian believers that this transformation *comes from the Lord.* Jenny bears responsibility for her own faith journey,[142] but ultimately the work of transformation is from God. This is both His promise and His plan. He will finish the work that was begun at the day of salvation, but it will not happen overnight. This is the journey of a lifetime.

If you, like Jenny, are overwhelmed at the thought of "doing it all," I would encourage you to relax. Be diligent. Be faithful. Keep at it. But relax. This *becoming Eve* puzzle *is* complicated and challenging. It is not for the faint of heart but there is no clock ticking on your progress and you are not alone. The Lord, who is the Spirit, is at work in you.

141 2 Corinthians 3:18
142 Philippians 2:12

Hope for the Future

Jenny's youthful enthusiasm for becoming a godly woman in her home is refreshing partly because she does not yet have much experience with failure. Atrocious chicken dinners notwithstanding, this young wife is blissfully unencumbered by the weight of years of sin and disappointment.

Most of us are not so guiltless. The idea of being transformed, while hopeful, is easily hampered by the haunting memory of failure, both in the recent and distant past. Perhaps you are not paralyzed by a daunting picture of the future, but it is the regret of the past that threatens to defeat you. I get that. My journey to discover and embrace the theology of biblical womanhood did not begin until I was almost fifty, with close to thirty years of marriage behind me. The reminders of my rebellion were fresh and sometimes overwhelming.

As I sat with my son early in his new-found faith journey and talked with him about being raised in a home where his dad's spiritual influence was compromised by my arrogance, I was almost overwhelmed by a sobering sense of sorrow for my own failure and sin. Even as I write these words I am threatened with despair again. That conversation initiated a work of the Holy Spirit in my soul that continues to inform every single day of my life. After a few days of despair, God gave me a renewed hope and a vision for what could be. The words of Joel 2:25 resonated in my spirit for weeks: "*I will restore to you the years that the swarming locust has eaten*" and I took hold of that promise, claiming its truth for my marriage, for the families of both of my children in the future, and for whatever ministry influence I might have.

Do you have a history that is marked by unbiblical womanhood? Is your memory full of conversations, decisions, and scenarios that now make you cringe? If you do, we are sisters.

What do we do with this failure?

We believe the promise of God in Romans 8:29. As we think about hardship and failure, we (the evangelical Christian church) love to quote Romans 8:28: *"And we know that for those who love God, all things work together for good, for those who are called according to His purpose."* In light of Paul's words, we might appropriately conclude my story with the statement that "God will work my failure for His good." And that's true. But, most people argue, how can my years of rebellion in my marriage have been good for Chas, or for me, or for our children? The disappointment and missed opportunities don't *feel good* at all.

Romans 8:28 is true, and we need to cling to its promise. But it is only half the equation. What we often miss is the next verse, where Paul *defines good*: *"For those whom He foreknew he also predestined* ***to be conformed to the image of His Son.****"* The complete thought from Romans 8 with regard to hardship and failure is that God works all things together for the conforming of His people to the image of His Son. *That* is His definition of "good."

The expressions of failure and sin in our lives are gathered up by the Savior and used by Him to conform us into His image. They are, each one, a part of our faith-journey *(being transformed!)* with God so that we are – more and more – conformed to the image of His Son. Which brings Him glory and brings us great joy.

When God graciously revealed my sin, I wept tears of regret and shame and disappointment. Since that day, my great passion has been to invite the Spirit to *correct* the bent of my own soul and to conform me into the image of God that was part of my original creation design. I am single-minded in my desire to *become Eve.* A HELPer and a life-giver.

Even in my failure.

What do we do with failure? We repent and believe that God will use even our sin as a means to conform us. The swarming locusts will not win. This is, after all, ultimately about our faithful God. He *will redeem those years.* It's a promise!

Hope for a Fresh Start

My daughter is a gymnastics coach. Having been a gymnast for more than ten years, she has had her share of forgotten routines, missed tumbling passes and less-than-graceful landings. She fell. She over-rotated. She lost her balance. She missed the "release." But Hannah's coach taught her to *use* the failure to learn something. To adjust. To focus. To tighten up. To loosen up. With few exceptions, crying was not an appropriate response to failure. The response to failure was *correction.*

One of the reasons that I have such affection and respect for the Apostle Paul is that he learned this exercise: repent, believe and *correct.* Surely this was one of the reasons that God called Paul to Himself. Never was there a man (at least from a human perspective) with a life marked more by disastrous failure and sin than Saul of Tarsus, hunter and persecutor of the early church and its young members. And yet, his life is a shining example of his own teaching in Romans 8! God used all the things together – disastrous *and* good – for the conforming of Saul, aka Paul, to His own image.

But the Apostle offers another principle for redemptive thinking about failure in the context of our being transformed into the image of God. He urges the church at Philippi: *"But one thing I do: forgetting what lies behind and straining toward what lies ahead, I press on toward the goal."* [143] While I am certain that

143 Philippians 3:14

there was much for Paul to learn from his history of rebellion, and I am sure that he exercised the discipline to repent and believe, I have the sense that he had refined the art of Gospel-driven amnesia. The art of *forgetting*, leaving at the cross the finished work of redemption so that he might make forward progress.

This principle is illustrated as the Lord sends out the Israelite people, finally making their way into the land of Canaan. After forty years of wandering, the people were at last on the brink of taking hold of the Promised Land. As they prepared to cross the Jordan River, the officers went through the camp and commanded the people: *"As soon as you see the ark of the covenant of the Lord your God being carried by the Levitical priests, then you shall set out from your place and follow it."*[144] When should they set out? *As soon as the Lord passed by them to lead the way.* **Do not look back.**

What if the Israelites had lingered, paralyzed by their own sense of failure and sin (which was legitimate, given their forty-year exile as a penalty for the collective sins of the nation)? What if they felt the need to erect an altar, offer just one more sacrifice, put on sackcloth and ashes to prove their sincere repentance? We might have thought them pious and humble. We would have understood their persistent remorse. How many times had they grumbled? How often had they forgotten the Lord? How hasty they were to worship other gods!

But God said, "Go now." Make forward progress. Now.

Had they failed? Yes. Repeatedly. But that failure was done and God had, in His mercy, forgiven them. The "looking back" season was over. They were beginning again, a fresh start, and it was time to *move*.

144 Joshua 3:3

Sometimes, as we reflect on our own failure and sin, whether regarding our gender or any other area of our lives, we are tempted to be paralyzed by guilt and self-recrimination. We repent. We believe that God can use our failure, but we are derailed for the future by fear and shame. This, sisters, is not from God. It is *possible* to love Jesus and still struggle with feelings of condemnation, but to do so is to live in bondage instead of freedom – and it is for freedom that Christ died![145] If you have confessed your sin to God in faith, believing that God is exactly who He says He is, then God will not treat you as your sins deserve. Instead, He will lavish you with mercy, forgiveness and love. Your sin, as far as the Father is concerned, has been removed! Consider this promise of God in Christ:

"He does not deal with us according to our sins, nor repay us according to our iniquities. For as high as the heavens are above the earth, so great is his steadfast love toward those who fear him; as far as the east is from the west, so far does He remove our transgressions from us. As a father shows compassion to his children, so the Lord shows compassion to those who fear him." [146]

If you are afraid that God's forgiveness does not extend to *your* sins, because they are so pervasive, so serious, so heinous, then this psalm is for you. It was true for Saul the predator. It is true for me. It is true for you.

It is good for me to have the tenderness to see my own heart and realize how quickly it can turn toward my own desires.[147] But I must not get stuck there, marinating in my own failure. Confession is a delight to the Savior. A refusal to accept His forgiveness is an affront. Be very careful here. We certainly bring nothing to the table of grace except our sin: no righteousness, no

145 Galatians 5:1
146 Psalm 103:10-12
147 Psalm 139:23-25

ability to pay Him back, no boasting. But that is the way God asks us to come. *And then He fills us up with grace, peace, hope, joy and* freedom. And we, with the Apostle Paul, are able to forget what is behind and strain toward what is ahead.

Jesus sums this up in Luke 9:62, *"No one who puts his hand to the plow [joins me in my work] and looks back is fit for the kingdom of God."* What do we do with failure? We lay it at the foot of the cross and receive the grace and mercy of God. We repent, believe and *correct*.

And we move on.

The Aroma of Christ

You can't see it, but "fragrance" permeates the air. Motivated home-sellers will often bake cookies, pulling them out of the oven just moments before an expected buyer arrives. Restaurants install fans in strategic locations to force the smell of baking bread, simmering sauces or perfectly grilled steaks out of the kitchen and into the atmosphere around prospective customers. Flower gardens, fish stalls, hospitals. Each has its particular and distinct smell. Aroma. Silently and without any visible evidence of its presence, it leaks out and fills the air.

The idea of the power of fragrance is not new to our generation. It seems that the pervasive nature of *smell* was characteristic of Paul's experience as well. Without much effort or information, our sanctified imagination can easily imagine a Mediterranean market – spices in the air, exotic flowers, and incense as well as the less enticing scent of animals (dead or alive), sweat and refuse. This idea of inescapable aroma served as a rich object lesson for the church at Corinth:

"But thanks be to God, who in Christ always leads us in triumphal procession, and through us spreads the fragrance of the knowl-

edge of Him everywhere. For we are the aroma of Christ to God among those who are being saved and among those who are perishing, to one a fragrance from death to death, to the other a fragrance from life to life."[148]

The terms used here for "aroma" are often used in the Greek to refer to the aroma of an actual sacrifice that is pleasing to God. The aroma of the sacrifice offered by Jesus makes its way into the marketplace not by way of spices and incense and exotic flowers. No. The aroma of the Gospel makes its way to those who are *being saved* by the very lives of those who love Christ. It leaks out of them and fills the air with the fragrance of grace. And mercy. And hope. And love.

Which begs the question: What is the aroma that leaks out of *me*? Whatever it is, for better or for worse, is an expression of the condition of my soul and it demonstrates itself by the qualities of my mind and character, my nature, constitution and makeup. This is my *disposition*. Without any visible evidence of its presence, it leaks out and fills the air.

This is why the distinction between doing and being as a godly woman is so significant. I – like Jenny – can attempt to do all the right things, check all the boxes of what I think it means to be a helper, but what is in my soul *leaks out of me*. The aroma of my heart and mind permeates the environment. Is it the aroma of a full life (past, present, and future!) sacrificed to God in Christ and demonstrated by my growing capacity for *ezer*-image bearing? Or is it the fragrance of self-protection, self-preservation, self-promotion? What do people see (and smell)?

Jerusalem, Judea, Samaria and Beyond!

Why does all of this matter and what does it have to do with

148 2 Corinthians 2:14-16

the puzzle of biblical womanhood? In short, we need to get a grip on the pervasive, all-encompassing, extensive and persistent ways that this new thinking informs our lives and ministries. The theology of gender, of womanhood in particular, is not relegated to marriage and mothering. These are important areas of application of godly womanhood. But the context for becoming a godly woman is not limited to homemaking.

Before His ascension to the right hand of the Father, Jesus urged His disciples to be His witnesses in Jerusalem, Judea and Samaria, and to the end of the earth.[149] This was a strategic initiative that would begin in their hometown and extend beyond the city of Jerusalem to the surrounding countryside and, eventually, to the world.

Similarly, my witness for Christ *begins* in my home. It is the most intimate arena to be filled with the aroma of Christ by the overflow of the soul of a godly woman. These people, more than any other, are deeply affected by my faith because it leaks profusely here. I make little effort to patch up the gaps and the air of our home is permeated by my disposition. What does that look like? How are their lives impacted for the Gospel by my womanhood?

Paul's letter to Titus urges women to be *"helpers* at home," a phrase which has been both wildly misused and casually dismissed. Paul's intent is often missed because of our own misinformation and prejudice. But the truth cannot be ignored simply because it is challenging. Remember that ultimately we want to be women whose lives are defined by the Word, so our responsibility is to seek to understand Paul's meaning rather than disregard it.

149 Acts 1:8

Single friends, you are not off the hook here. We are talking about "Jerusalem" as a home and *a family* and I know that you are tempted to 1) tune out and 2) become discouraged as you are reminded, yet again, that you do not have a "family." May I gently encourage you to hang on? While it is true that becoming a helper in the context of a home is significant as it relates to husbands and wives and mothers and their children, two important principles come to mind here.

First, being a helper is not limited to the relationship between men and women. John Piper, in his work *What's the Difference*, writes: "There may be occasions when women have no interaction with men [husbands] and yet are still mature in their femininity. This is because femininity is a disposition to affirm, not just experience." It is imperative that you think about your womanhood, your unique femininity, in light of *all* of your life and relationships. This includes your parents and grandparents and your siblings, but it also includes your roommates, coworkers, teammates, pastors and elders, and friends. All of them. Men *and* women.

Second, the writer of Proverbs 31 makes an interesting and easily overlooked point in his description of the "excellent wife." *"She does him [her husband] good, not harm,* all the days of her life." Do you see that? She does him good **all the days of her life.** In other words, the excellent wife has been "doing her husband good" *even before she knew him.* That means that every day – even the lonely days long before a wedding is on the visible horizon – she is living with him in mind, whoever "he" may turn out to be! Much could be said about all that such thinking suggests, but for our purposes, let's focus on the effort to cultivate this HELPer disposition during this season so that, should the Lord bring you a husband, you will be a *lifegiver* from the very beginning. It will not be easy, but this is an opportunity for you to see the steadfast love of the Lord, to grow in your confidence in His plan for your life and to wait not passively, but with purpose and intent.

This is our Jerusalem. What is the fragrance that fills the air here? Do we need to open a window, or is the aroma *life-giving*? Let's look at this aspect of ezer-living, that of our Jerusalem Refuge closely in Chapter 9.

Beyond Jerusalem is the area of Judea and Samaria. For the Apostles, Jesus' instruction was meant to spur them on beyond the comforts of home. For our purpose, in the context of the consideration of godly womanhood, we will look beyond the home to the church, as it is the second "layer" of relational intimacy for the Christ-follower.

I am aware that the validity of church affiliation is under scrutiny, if not outright attack, by evangelicals today. Such teaching is deeply distressing – to the point of being heretical[150] – but I do not intend to use this text as a means to correct that line of thinking. Living together, doing life and worshipping with other flawed, sinful, rebellious people is incredibly difficult but it is the means that God has appointed for us to become mature disciples of Christ and it is to this church that we will speak with regard to godly womanhood.

We will carefully consider the fragrance of godly womanhood as it permeates the air in the Tabernacle of Faith in Chapter 10.

Finally, Jesus instructed His followers to take the Gospel to the *ends of the earth*. Those men took that admonition seriously and, as a result of their Spirit-filled obedience, the church spread

150 All of the Pastoral Epistles affirm both explicitly and implicitly the absolute import of church affiliation to the Christian's maturity and faithful expression of Christ-likeness.

throughout the known world over the next fifty years. It was an amazing expedition of faith.

So how does the aroma of godly womanhood drift from your home and your church into the atmosphere of school, work, recreation, neighborhoods and culture? Remember in Chapter 3 we determined that *becoming Eve*, an *ezer*-helper, has application for every season and circumstance of our lives. This beyond-home-and-church thinking is challenging, particularly as we think about the culture, politics, the boardroom, and the broader global community. However, notwithstanding the challenge, this arena of our feminine expression has great opportunity for Kingdom impact.

Acts 17:26 affirms God's specific plan for where the *helper* would live. *"He made from one man every nation of mankind to live on all the face of the earth, having determined allotted periods* ***and the boundaries of their dwelling place.*** *"* There she sleeps, and eats, and works, and worships for a reason. What does it mean to be *uniquely feminine here*? In my neighborhood? At my office? In the world?

Good question. We'll consider this aspect of godly womanhood in Chapter 11.

A Puzzle of Immense Proportion

The four corners: Hedge protector. Empathizer. Lifter. Promoter.

Eve. Sarah. Abraham. David, the Shepherd-King. Mary's sister, Martha. Paul. Thomas. The man by the pool. Jeremiah in the well. Peter. Moses. Aaron. Elijah.

Hannah. Milas. Chas. My mom. My sister. Maria. My friends Tracy and Sarah and Beth and Brittney and Jill. The Grinch.

The Rehab Addict. The Nuremberg defendants.

These are the straight edges. And they're all put together. What's next?

We have tumblers full of colorful pieces that hold the promise of an exquisitely illustrated picture. Its likeness is found in the pages of Scripture and in the stories of God's faithfulness to His people over thousands of years. As we begin to turn them over and fit them together, what appeared to be myriad random pieces will become a beautiful scene full of color and patterns and glorious detail. This is a puzzle of immense proportion. Be inspired and encouraged as the pieces are rightly arranged and fit together. Let's go forward, remembering these words from the very beginning: "And it was *very* good."

Chapter Nine

THE HELPER REFUGE

Home. It's where the heart is. There's no place like it. It's a man's castle. Well, at least it is for Prince William and his royal family. Their Apartment 1a of Kensington Palace is a four-story home, with up to thirty rooms and nine bathrooms. And that's just their London residence.

Being a "royal" has its perks.

Personally, I'm content with the home that we've lived in for more than twenty years. There's always something that needs to be done, but we raised our children here and it is the place where I am most comfortable and at peace. I have a few favorite spots, like my rocking chair by the fireplace and my grandmother's chair in front of the bay window in our bedroom. I love our porch and our sunroom. This home is an expression of God's love and faithfulness to our family and I am grateful.

What exactly do we mean when we talk about *becoming Eve* in the context of "home"? For many people, "home" is synonymous with "family." For others, "home" has a broader application. It may include extended family, roommates, and pets. As we consider how to apply what we have learned about biblical womanhood, each of these definitions is relevant.

Remember that God's design for His daughters is more about *personhood* than about role. It is one aspect of her *disposition*, which the Oxford Dictionary defines as "a person's inherent qualities of mind and character". The dictionary offers these synonyms for "disposition": temperament, nature, constitution and makeup. So we are not talking primarily about what we "do" in our Jerusalem, our home. We are asking the Holy Spirit to change *who we are*. And that has implications for immediate family relationships, roommates, extended family and even (I suppose) for pets.

The Adam Family

Introduced to us in Genesis, we're familiar with Adam and Eve, Dad and Mom. God gave them to each other as a gift, and even after their banishment from Eden, the Lord continued to bless them. They had three sons: Cain, Abel and Seth.

However, theirs was not a fairy-tale ending. In fact, one brother murdered the other in a fit of jealousy. Even so, it is significant to note that this was God's design for His people: that man and woman would marry, have children and live together for better or for worse.

Let's clarify this important detail relative to *family* in the Kingdom of God. In every instance throughout all of Scripture, all sixty six books and every one of the hundreds of chapters, when people marry and have a family, the union is between a *man* and a *woman*.

Noah and Mrs. Noah.[151]

Abraham and Sarah.

Isaac and Rebekah.

Boaz and Ruth.

Elkanah and Hannah.

Zechariah and Elizabeth.

151 She's not named, but they had three sons so it is safe to assume Noah was married to a woman. Additionally, God refers to Noah's wife in Genesis 6:18.

Joseph and Mary.

Aquilla and Priscilla.

Man. Woman. Every single time. Yes, this historically accepted principle is being challenged and, indeed, has been legally set aside by the highest court in our country. But in the economy of the Sovereign King of the Universe, a *family* begins with a husband and a wife.

While the legalization of same-sex marriage represents the extreme morphing of the traditionally defined family, there are other, more mainstream changes in the landscape of "family" that have an impact on our thinking relative to womanhood. Once characterized by TV's Ward and June Cleaver who, together with Wally and Beaver gathered every evening around the dinner table for a home-cooked meal served on real china and with actual linens, "the family" in America is no longer quite so predictable. Ward's strong fatherly presence at the head of the table, softened and tempered by June's gracious affection and sense of humor, is indicative of an era not long past, yet all but extinct. The scene around the dinner table represented only a glimpse of the Cleaver family dynamic, but it was a window into their lives. In some ways, the same is true of our homes today.

Never seeming to stress or sweat or become angry, June was the epitome of motherhood for that generation. The more contemporary mom has traded in her pearls and kitten heel pumps for a power suit and running gear, and dinner is often drive-through or take-out. While June Cleaver's biggest challenge was getting the boys to wash their hands before dinner, today's mom often balances conference calls, business trips, and sales quotas in addition to laundry, grocery runs, baseball practice, violin lessons, field trips, teacher/parent meetings and church. Having dinner together, actually gathering around the table for a home-cooked meal, happens so rarely in many families that it is relegated to Easter, Thanksgiving and Christmas.

Working moms. Traveling dads. Busy kids. Blended families. Single friends sharing the rent. Family life is complicated. The competing dynamics of marriage, children, work, school, and church have never been so demanding. What's a godly woman to do? Making time for a few minutes alone with the Lord in His Word often seems like a luxury – or a chore. The list of things to do, to remember, to prepare seems never ending and the effort just to keep going from one day to the next is monumental. Most of us are grateful to fall into bed in the evening without having had a new crisis arise. *How is it going to be possible to add "be a helper" to the list of responsibilities at home?*

An Unlikely Helper

Once upon a time, there was a beautiful woman who lived in a wall. She lived by herself, but she was rarely alone. Men – even to the rank of king – came and went throughout the day and night and the woman became infamous for her services.

One day, two strangers arrived at her doorstep. These men were foreigners. They came not for her services but for shelter, for they were spies who were being hunted by the King's men. The woman hid the spies and lied to the soldiers who sought them out, saving the strangers from certain execution. "Why have you done this for us?" the men asked as soon as the gates closed, assuring their safety. "I know about the Lord and I know He is to be feared. Whatever you do, please be kind to me and to my family – my father and mother and brothers and sisters – and deliver us from the calamity that surely awaits our city."

And so they did.

This CliffsNotes® version of the story of Rahab[152] sets up a radical illustration of biblical womanhood in the context of family. The account of her family is very brief; indeed, they are mentioned only in Joshua 2:12 & 13, 6:22-25. They are lumped together as her "father's household." We do not have much information about her history or the dynamics of her relationship to her family. But we can guess. Surely, even in Jericho, it was not every man's dream for his little girl to become a prostitute – even one highly paid with well-respected clientele.

Picture the scene as Rahab leaves her home and quickly makes her way through the streets of Jericho to her father's house to warn him of the impending danger. Once she explains the events that led her to their living room, Rahab likely endures the scorn and anger of her father and brothers. She is already an embarrassment to their family. Now, her actions have been tantamount to *treason* and they are all at risk.

But Rahab must have stood her ground. Very new to the faith, and without any personal history with the God of Israel, she testified with confidence *and* humility to His power and His mercy. In her book *Unashamed*, Francine Rivers describes how that conversation might have been exchanged:

"What are these walls to a God who can part the seas? Have you ever heard of such power? Truly, He is God, the *only* God ...You must decide where to place your faith, father. You can have faith in the King of Jericho, who is but a man. Or you can put your faith in the King of Kings, the God of Israel ... [but] we have one chance, and that chance rests in the Lord God of Israel."[153]

While Rivers' account is fictional, we know from Scripture

152 From Joshua 2 & 6
153 Rivers, *Unashamed*, excerpts from p. 51-54

that Rahab somehow managed to convince her family to take shelter in her home as Jericho was surrounded by the Israelites. The spies were true to their word and they rescued Rahab, her father and mother, brothers and sisters and *"all who belonged to her"*[154] even as the walls that housed her home began to tumble around them. This story has a happy ending, as Rahab and her father's household were adopted into the family of God, and Rahab became only one of five women named in the lineage of Christ. (Spoiler alert: she married one of the spies. Doesn't that have the makings of a great movie?)

Rahab the Ezer

Think about Rahab in the context of what we have learned from God's Word about His *ezer*-image.

From Psalm 33:20, we recall that God is our Hedge of Protection: *"Our soul waits for the Lord for He is our ezer and our shield."*

From Psalm 86:17, *"O Lord, you have ezer-ed (helped) me and comforted me"* we know that God Empathizes with us and knows our needs.

From Psalm 20:2, we see the Lifting and sustaining nature of God: *"May He send you ezer from the sanctuary and grant you support from Zion."*

Finally, from Psalm 89, we are reminded that God will promote His purposes and plans for our lives: *"I have granted ezer to one who is mighty; I have exalted one chosen from the people."*

Do you see how God displayed His own *ezer* character and nature in His relationship with Rahab? It was God who

154 Joshua 6:25

protected her. It was God who knew her needs, her fears, her hopes and dreams. It was God who would sustain her and give her courage. It was God who orchestrated all of the details so that His plans and purposes for her life (and her family and, ultimately the Savior!) would not be thwarted.

Now consider how Rahab, *very young in her walk with God,* began to "mirror" the image of the *ezer* Helper God in her relationship with her family. Again, we have little specific information about how Rahab lived among her family prior to this scene in Joshua 2 and virtually nothing to tell us how she got them to agree to come to her home for shelter. But whatever the details, we can surmise these few things about Rahab's heart and mind as she set about the task of rescuing her family:

Rahab provided physical protection for her family, at significant risk to her own safety. She was proactive, caring for *"all who belonged to her"* by bringing them into her own home and including them in the promise that God had made through the spies to rescue her. She provided for them a **Hedge of protection** and in doing so pointed her family to God, her *ezer* and her shield.

She **Empathized** with the plight of those who were at risk and entered into their experience by aligning herself with them. Keep in mind that Rahab could have kept a low profile, maintained her distance and thus saved herself with minimal risk and effort. Instead, she stepped outside of her own circumstance and entered the world of her family *so that they might be saved.* Her empathy illustrated for them the God who does not stand far off, removed and distant from the agony of His children but instead delivers ultimate comfort that would lead to abundant and eternal life.

Rahab offered support and sustaining grace to family members who, in all likelihood, had written her off. Remember the analogy of the house threatened by "lateral disintegration"? [155] Without strong support from the internal structure, the house would crumble. Who would have expected such support to come to Rahab's family through the person of the prostitute? But that's exactly what happened. She knew and understood their plight, but she would not leave them there. She gave them courage and hope from her own small faith. With God at work in her, Rahab *became* the **Lifter,** the strong column of support that her family needed to endure, indeed to survive, the disaster that would come on their city.

Lastly, Rahab knew that God had a plan and purpose for her family and she set out to **Promote** His agenda with no clear understanding of what that might even mean for them. What would a family of Jericho-ites *do* with no place to call home? How would they be accepted by the conquerors (or would they)? What would their future hold? Rahab had no answers to these questions, but she had an elementary understanding of the nature of God and she knew that He would be faithful. He who had rescued a tiny nation from the empire of Egypt by the parting of the Sea? Yes. This God would accomplish His plans and purposes for their lives, and she would be like Him.

As you ponder the illustration of Rahab, it is tempting to get sidetracked by what she *did.* Which is not insignificant. But the actions taken by Rahab overflowed from the faith given to her by the God of Israel. Consider her testimony from Joshua 2:9-11:

"I know that the Lord has given you the land, and that the fear of you has fallen upon us, and that all the inhabitants of the land melt

155 Chapter 6

away before you. For we have heard how the Lord dried up the water of the Red Sea before you when you came out of Egypt, and what you did to the two kings of the Amorites who were beyond the Jordan, to Sihon and Og, whom you devoted to destruction. And, as soon as we heard it, our hearts melted, and there was no spirit left in any man because of you, for the Lord your God, he is God in the heavens above and on the earth beneath."

This woman had no spiritual advantage. She had no history or heritage of faith. No feast days or Sabbath. No temple worship or sacrifice. She had not had the benefit of the teaching of the priests or the prophets. Her faith, declared in that first statement, "*I* know *that the* Lord *has given you the land*." was a supernatural gift of the Spirit and it seeped into her heart and mind in such a way that she began to be transformed in that very moment. The Spirit of the Lord was transforming her. She was becoming the woman that God intended her to be, in the heat of a very chaotic and frightening situation.

What a testimony to the faithfulness of God and the work of His Holy Spirit in a woman to help her to *become Eve*. The woman that He designed and intended for her to be. A Helper in the context of her home.

An Unlikely Home

It's easy to miss, but notice that Rahab, who was an *ezer* in her Jerusalem home, *was not married.* She demonstrated her *ezer* disposition in the context of her own circumstance, tainted and unlikely as it was, but she was not married and she did not have children.

As we begin to think practically about *ezer* living in our Jerusalem homes, Rahab's story ought to inform our perspective. Godly womanhood, applied to the family, will include those intimate relationships of wives to husbands and mothers to children. But it also takes into account extended family members and others who live in close proximity to you. I love the way that Scripture defines Rahab's family as *"all who belonged to her."* That's helpful for married people and women who are single.

Where is your Jerusalem? It is the arena of your most intimate relationships, the people who are related to you by marriage or blood and those to whom you are "knit" by circumstance. It may be described by *all who belong to you.* Let's look at the disposition of godly womanhood from this vantage point, using the terms "family" and "home" with Rahab's story in mind.

A Hedge Protector at Home

When we think about having the disposition of a hedge protector, we can tend to focus primarily on physical security, which is obviously important. My grandson, who is just beginning to pull himself along in the army crawl on the floor, has a vantage point to see things that big people tend to miss. Like little bits of paper, a single pumpkin seed, or (on rare occasions) dirt. Every discovery makes its way from his little fingers to his mouth, but so far (at least as far as we know) we have managed to extract each foreign object before he swallowed . We want our home to be a safe place for Micah.

But being a helper/hedge-protector is more than creating an environment that is "danger-free." When you think about feeling "safe," what other words come to your mind? How about words like calm, order, quiet, and rest? As you think about *those* words, how might your disposition of godly womanhood inform the environment of your home? This aspect of *becoming Eve* expresses itself uniquely in every home, but the effect is that, when people walk in the door they are able to take a deep sigh of relief.

My mother's home was like that. It was not perfectly ordered or spotlessly clean. It did not look like a magazine cover. She had a lot of *stuff* and every shelf, wall, nook and cranny was a display for some knickknack that had meaning to her or to my grandmother (who lived with my mom for fifteen years). But my mom's house was a refuge, for me and for my siblings and our children, but really for anyone who came in her door. Often, as I walked into her house, I felt the urge to sigh "Ahhhhh." It literally was a place where it seemed like the burden of the *outside* stayed *outside.*

How does that happen? It is important to acknowledge that we cannot possibly say what this means for every woman and every home. But it must mean at least that the *people who belong to us* are not surrounded by unnecessary clutter, the constant clamor of noise (think television, video games, loud music) or the chaos of half-finished projects. The dependability of routine cultivates security. Keeping the dust and cobwebs at bay and the refrigerator free of spoiled food allows the godly woman to relax alongside the people that she loves.

These things are not complicated and they don't have to be done perfectly. A home that is a refuge will be much more than a clutterless, quiet, orderly and clean box with four walls. But these few examples come from the overflow of the heart and mind of a godly woman who, however she accomplishes it, longs for *all who belong to her* – husband, children, in-laws, roommates, or traveling friends – to be safe and secure in her home.

I love the words of the Savior from John 16:33 *"I have said these things to you that in me you may have peace. In the world, you will have tribulation. But take heart, I have overcome the world."*

It is instructive to remind ourselves that those who belong to us are in the world daily, and in the world there is tribulation. In contrast, our homes ought to resonate with the peace of Christ. This is a place where people can be rested and refreshed. To a great degree, sisters, this is a reflection of our *becoming Eve*. As we prayerfully and thoughtfully examine ourselves and our environment, we should expect the Holy Spirit to expose those aspects of our lives and homes that need to be adjusted. This is part of our *being transformed*.

Safe to Be Real

Remember, however, that there is another aspect of hedge protecting that is less about "place" and more about "person." As you think about *all those who belong to you*, do they feel safe with you? Safe to be frustrated. Safe to be angry. Safe to be weary. Safe to be disappointed. Are they able to be vulnerable? Do they hold back from you out of fear of your disapproval, or dismissal, or disdain?

In order to graduate from his Christian high school, my son was required to write a paper defining his "Statement of Faith." He was, however, in the midst of a very difficult season with regard to his faith and he refused to write what he did not believe. He wrote a paper that was titled "Why I Don't Believe." I still think it was a credit to this school and to his teachers that they allowed Milas to make this choice, but it was heart-wrenching for me. As I read that paper, I felt deeply saddened. I wrestled with my own failure and feared for my son's salvation. But I was grateful, and am grateful to this day, that Milas felt the freedom to express his opinion (respectfully) even as it was diametrically opposed to everything we had taught him.[156]

156 You already know the end of this story: this paper was just one tool used by

A brief word to wives. (Single sisters, file this away!) Your husband manages a great deal of responsibility and stress, regardless of his profession. One aspect of our *ezer* design is our refusal to make that more difficult by having unrealistic and unfair expectations of him. Live within your means, not requiring more of him than he can reasonably provide. Be thoughtful about what you expect from him at home. Should he be engaged with you and with the children and with your home life? Absolutely. But think carefully about what that means for your family.

I am probably going out on a limb here, but in our current evangelical culture, we have a pretty high expectation that dads lead devotions at the dinner table, or with the children at bedtime. And in the early days of our marriage, that's exactly what I thought (hence my disappointment after that fateful Advent devotion). The idea that a father lead devotions for his family is admirable. But is it necessarily biblical? Ummmm....no. The principle of fathers training their children *is biblical*[157]. The application that they "lead family devotions" at the dinner table or some other set time is from James Dobson (whom I love, by the way)? Not from Jesus. Please be *very careful* that your expectations of your husband in this regard and others are not more than he can manage. Do not set him up for failure. *He must be safe with you!*

Becoming Eve means that I am always asking the Lord if there are ways that I should carefully tend my place and personhood as a hedge of protection around *all who belong to me.* As I do so, I exercise the discipline to believe that God is my *shield* and *defender*. Because He is my contender, I am able to think less about myself and more about the benefit of those around me. It is His help that has saved me.

God to draw Milas to himself. Hallelujah!
157 Deuteronomy 6

In the same way, I know that ultimately God is the *shield* and *defender* for *all who belong to me.* I cannot protect them from everything, nor should I. As an *ezer*/hedge-protector, I need to exercise my faith in the work of God in their lives. I remind myself, and I remind those who belong to me, that *"Our soul waits for the Lord for He is our ezer and our shield."*

Becoming an Empathizer at Home

It ought to be easy to "remember what it was like" as I engage with my children. I ought to remember my broken heart, my failing tests and papers, the temptation to skip class, to lie and to cheat. It should not be hard to recall wrecked cars, embarrassing pimples and miserable hair days. But in the season of raising my children, I was easily distracted by my own challenges and issues and "remembering" takes time. In his little booklet, *The Duties of Parents*, J. C. Ryle describes this as "a willingness to enter into childish troubles, a readiness to take part in childish joys."[158] Sounds simple, but for most of us, this "remembering" thing is tedious.

I was sitting with a group of women doing a Bible study one summer when we somehow sidetracked to talking about our adolescent children. At one point, I remember remarking about some disappointment with Hannah. My sweet friend Cindi said to me, very kindly, "Susan, you are expecting Hannah to think and act like *you* would – except that you have had twenty years of experience with the Lord to inform you. You have got to think about Hannah in terms of her *very young walk with God!*" That was so helpful for me. If I could only *remember* my own heart and mind, and the challenges that I faced at Hannah's age I would have been sobered by my own immaturity and much

158 J. C.. Ryle, *The Duties of Parents*, Triangle Press, 1888, 1996. Page 4

less inclined to be dismissive of my daughter.

Remember what it was like. To be afraid. To be disappointed. To be insecure. To be lonely.

The other side of the empathy coin is the ability to become a woman who seeks to understand those who are not at all like her. This requires the refining of our ability to ask good questions – and our exercise of patience to wait for and listen to the answers.

An obvious application of this disposition is in marriage. It is reasonable to conclude that our God-designed differences have the potential to be the source of marital distress. Women see things differently than men. We value different things. We manage challenges differently. We communicate differently. Every family has its own version of this dynamic, but the principle is the same in every home. And these differences apply to seasons of grief, joy, stress, fear, and crisis. Given this challenge, a woman who is *becoming Eve*, being transformed into the image of her *ezer* God, must make understanding a priority.

Toward that end, be more *curious* than certain. Listen more than you talk, and ask good, thoughtful questions of your husband, questions like:

What do you wish that you could change about your life?

What worries you?

What do you love about your job? What would you change if you could?

What would you like to be doing in five years? Ten years?

How have I encouraged you recently?

How have I *discouraged* you?

One of our challenges is that we assume that we know the

answers to these questions. And maybe we do. The issue is not just the *knowing*, it's engaging in the conversation so that **he knows you are interested.** That's the heart of a godly woman who is an empathizer. And who knows, you might find out something that surprises you!

This "seeking to understand" effort is not limited to the relationship between husbands and wives! There are numerous scenarios, as we think about *all who belong to us* to whom it will apply.

Do you have a roommate who hates to cook – and you subscribe to four cooking magazines?

Do you have a child who struggles at school – and you were an easy "A" student?

Do you have a child who is not an athlete – and you lettered in four sports?

Do you have a mother-in-law who was an educator – and you have chosen to homeschool your children?

You see the point. Each of these people that we love are at risk of our judgment, based on our differences, unless we make the effort to seek to understand by listening more than we talk, asking strategic questions (go back to those curious questions we just asked – they apply!) and trusting the Holy Spirit to enlarge our capacity for empathy.

I want to be a woman who remembers, not so consumed with my present reality that I do not recall my own history for the benefit of those who are struggling. I want to *become* a woman who is willing to do the hard work to understand those whose experience is foreign to me.

Becoming Eve means that I remember the *ezer* God, who *"sympathizes with my weaknesses."* He is not surprised, or uninterested, or dismissive. Rather, He is moved to pity and compassion and, by His own choice, He enters into my suffering and shame – ultimately giving His *life* so that I will not be lost.

In the same way, I know that ultimately it is God who can empathize with *all who belong to me.* He understands them, even when I don't. As an *ezer*/empathizer, I need to exercise my confidence in the promises of God for the people that I love. I remind myself, and I remind those who belong to me, *"O Lord,* You *have helped me and comforted me."* What more do we need?

Becoming a Lifter at Home

We are in the process of planning a remodel in our kitchen. It was my hope that we could take down the wall between our kitchen and sunroom; however, when the contractor came out to look at the project, he informed me that the wall was "load bearing." It could not be removed without compromising the structure of the house. The solution that he suggested was to install columns to support the weight of the "load," opening up the room while taking care to provide the strong support needed structurally.

Becoming Eve in the context of home and family requires the providing of strong support and sustaining influence. This means that the helper/lifter is sensitive and alert to issues of vitality, health and strength from a physical *and* spiritual perspective.

As you think about *all those who belong to you*, what do they need to sustain their physical health? You might think in terms of nutrition, and exercise, and rest. These are areas where you have the opportunity to influence the people that you love by giving them good, healthy options for meals and snacks, encouraging them to be active by doing physical activities with them, and reminding them to rest by winding down the noise, action and energy at the appropriate time.

The effort to maintain balance is particularly difficult in our culture. There are so many *good* opportunities available to women and families and it often seems irresponsible to *not* take advantage of them. The temptation is to fill up every moment of every day with good, "productive" activity. That is the American way.

Years ago I read an account of a traveler who set out on an expedition in the heart of a very dense and treacherous jungle. He had hired a team of men who were native to the area to serve as his guides. The first few days, they made swift progress, and the man was pleased. On the third day, however, the guides rested well into the morning. When they finally awakened, they lingered over a meal and then, to the man's growing annoyance, sat down to rest, smoke a pipe and chatter for a while. Finally, the man inquired of the captain of the guides, "Why are we waiting here? For two days we have traveled quickly and made efficient progress. Why do we not move forward today?" "We have moved too fast," the guide replied. "Our bodies have gone swiftly, but we have left behind our soul. We wait today for our soul to catch us."[159]

How descriptive that is of our typical lives! We move so swiftly, we stay so busy doing *good things* that we leave our soul behind. The *ezer*/lifter is a woman who is thoughtful and deliberate about the schedule in her home. Together with her husband, she makes choices that ensure her family's vitality by choosing the best over the good, even when doing so is unpopular. A single sister must be equally committed to discerning choices, best over good, as she is often tempted to take advantage of every opportunity simply because the calendar is open. If

159 Paraphrased from Angela Guffey, *Tender Mercies for a Mother's Soul*

she is not careful, she too will leave behind her soul.

The woman who is an *ezer* offers not only sustaining support for health and vitality, but also the effort to lift those who belong to her out of despair, discouragement, and fear. When one falls into the pit, it is the godly woman who, in the image and nature of God, carefully puts those rags under her arms and gently lifts her out.

When we are struggling, we typically respond in one of two ways. We either look at life through our circumstances, or we look at life through the character and nature of God and how He cares for us. The disposition of godly womanhood leans toward the latter and lifts *all those who belong to her* to the same response.

This is the lens of *circumstantial* perspective:

> I did not make the team ... get that promotion ... get invited to that party.
>
> Everyone else has a date to the dance. If I go, I am going alone.
>
> I am afraid I will never get married.
>
> I cannot understand this material and I am going to fail my test.
>
> I am afraid to apply for that job.
>
> No one appreciates what I do at work.

Such complaints are often met with platitudes like:

> Don't worry. You can keep practicing and try out again next year.
>
> That promotion must not have been God's will for you. Let's be grateful for His direction.
>
> I am sure you will find someone to marry. You just have to be patient.
>
> Go for it! You have nothing to lose by trying!

These are responses that I am certain come from good intentions. They even seem like "lifter"-type responses. But take just a moment to consider, how *helpful* are these tried-and-true replies?

The reality is that our own advice, even if it's right and even if it comes from our experience, does not hold the power and promise that is afforded us in Scripture. *Becoming Eve* requires the exercise of asking the Lord to give us a new perspective, one that helps others to see life through the lens of His Word. It is here that we set our feet on the Truth and find solid, dependable ground to stand on.

Take just a minute to read Psalm 91. (Pausing for you to read.) What do you find in the words of the psalmist that helps you to answer the sampling of complaints that we listed? How about this:

> *Because he holds fast to me in love, I will* ***deliver*** *him;*
> *I will* ***protect*** *him because He knows my name.*
> *When he calls to me, I will* ***answer*** *him;*
> *I will* ***be with him*** *in trouble;*
> *I will* ***rescue*** *and* ***honor*** *him.*
> *With long life I will* ***satisfy*** *him and* ***show him my salvation****.*

Wow. Just those few verses from that incredible psalm inform our fear, despair, and discouragement and set us on a new path of hope.

I know that you did not make the team and that is really disappointing. But I want to remind you that God *promises* to honor you and to satisfy you. He knows your name. He is with you and will show you Himself even in this disappointment!

I know that you are afraid that you will never find someone to marry. I cannot guarantee that you will. But we have to remember, together, that when you call out to Him in fear and despair, God will answer you. He will be with you. He will satisfy you and show you His salvation – His plan for you!

As an *ezer-lifter*, these are the words breathe life into *all who belong to me*. It is these words that give hope and perspective. These are the words that have the power to lift the despondent out of the slough. Helping those that we love to depend on God's Word in the midst of their circumstance cultivates their theology, and *that* is life-giving!

Becoming Eve means that I remember that it is *ezer* God who *"sends help from the sanctuary and support from Zion."* It is God who sustains my life from one moment to the next. It is God who, in my deepest despair, lifts me from death to life.

In the same way, I know that ultimately it is God who will lift *all who belong to me*, sustaining their lives and giving them strong support. I am not able to manage every detail so that they are guaranteed health and vitality. I will often not say the right things, make the right choices, or be the encourager that they need. But they belong to God. He will send them help and support them. I can count on that.

Becoming a Promoter at Home

In our consideration of the theology of an ezer/promoter, we looked at the story of David and remarked that his was perhaps the original "Cinderella story." I have recently had the privilege of seeing the Broadway adaptation of the *real* "Cinderella." The musical was beautifully performed with stunning special effects. One nuance of the original that I noticed with fresh perspective at this performance was the vehemence with which Cinderella's stepmother held the girl captive in her own home. She was clearly aware of Cinderella's beauty and character and, rather than encourage her to blossom and grow, her stepmother insisted that she remain dressed in tatters, slaving away in their home.

Now, I know it's just a fairy tale, but any fool could see that Cinderella had "princess potential." I mean, not only did she have the look of a princess (even in tatters), she carried herself with poise, sang with the voice of an angel, and *talked to the animals*. Seriously, how could she *not* marry the prince?

A woman who is *becoming Eve* cultivates the ability to look for the "princess" in the people that she loves. Casting a vision for others, and helping people find and succeed in the good purpose that God has for their lives is a reflection of the *ezer*-promoter nature of God.

Timothy grew up in a home with a strong believing mother and grandmother, and a father who was Greek[160] (probably not a Christian). He was exposed to the Scripture *"in infancy."*[161] We do not know much more about his childhood and youth, but he so impressed Paul that the Apostle invited the young man, probably in his teens, to join him on his second missionary journey. Paul describes Timothy, his *"beloved and faithful child in the Lord,"*[162] as a man of sincere faith and of significant giftedness. Eventually, Timothy would assume a pastoral role in the church at Ephesus.

Can't you imagine that Timothy must have been every mother's dream? A dutiful, smart, strong, self-assured young man who impressed even the Apostle. Interestingly, as his story is revealed in clues throughout the Pastoral Epistles, we learn that Timothy was actually timid,[163] apparently not very strong

160 Acts 16:1
161 2 Timothy 3:14
162 1 Corinthians 4:17
163 2 Timothy 1:8

physically,[164] and insecure about his authority.[165] Without any more information than this, but with Paul's gracious affirmation of Lois and Eunice (Timothy's mother and grandmother, respectively), it is not a stretch to imagine that it was Lois who *promoted* the purpose and plan of God in Timothy's life. He does not appear to have been a "natural leader," powerful orator or winsome personality. But Lois must have seen in him what was *possible*, and surely she did all that she could to encourage the work of God in Timothy's life.

This is the disposition of a student, one who is interested in *all who belong to her*, studying them to discover and promote their strengths, passion, vision and potential.

What does she love?

What makes him sweat?

When does he "shine"?

What will she talk about, read about, study incessantly?

What makes her tired and easily discouraged?

Not distracted by what *is*, the *ezer* is able to see *what could be*. Toward that end, she is a cheerleader and a coach, a challenger and an instructor.

Sometimes, the ezer/promoter will press the one that she loves to take a risk, try something new, even if it means "failure." She encourages him to grow, to learn from experiences, and to not waste any criticism, good or bad. She offers opportunities, makes things possible, and does what she can to create pathways for potential development.

Other times, the woman who is *becoming Eve* will offer diffi-

164 1 Timothy 5:23
165 2 Timothy 1:6

cult truth, helping *all that belong to her* to be realistic, within the context of the Gospel. Proverbs 27:6 offers this insightful wisdom: *"Faithful are the wounds of a friend."* Without malice, godly womanhood demands integrity that exercises itself particularly with those whom she loves. This is risky but necessary. God has a plan and purpose for each of our lives; we must not wish for anything else. If our desires are consistent with His plan, He will equip us for the work that He has set before us. If we are ill equipped in a particular area, we ought to at least consider whether this is the place for God's plan to unfold.

However, our confidence comes from the knowledge that it is God who *"grants help...and exalts"* His people. This is true for my own life; He is at work to accomplish His purpose in me. As I resist the temptation to promote *myself*, trusting Him to finish the work that He began in me, I am free to promote His plans and purposes in the lives of *all who belong to me.*

Becoming Eve means that I long for those that I love to have a vision for their life that is inspiring and hopeful. I want to help them discover their strengths and gifts and passions and to grow in their areas of weakness. But I must acknowledge that I do not know the mind of God. I cannot and should not seek to control the lives of those that I love. I remind myself, and my loved ones, that ultimately it is God who will promote them in His own time and according to His plan.

Another Word to Wives (Single Sisters ... Do Not Dismiss This)

Becoming Eve, a helper/promoter, in the context of marriage to a man who is less spiritually mature than you is a particular challenge. It is not my intent to articulate a thorough argument for male headship in the home; others have done that with great expertise and after years of study. But the truth, based on all of Scripture and redemptive history, is that God created man, *men*, to be the leader in the home. He is the "head" of the household. Paul puts forth this point clearly in 1 Corinthians 11:7-9 and again in Ephesians 5. Wayne Grudem puts it this way: "Women are to honor...the special responsibility that God has given men in the spiritual leadership in the home.... Where male headship is not acknowledged, our functioning as the image of God is hampered and diminished."[166]

That said, what is a woman to do whose husband *will not* or *cannot* lead? This is a difficult issue to address universally. But there are some principles that ought to be embraced by ezer/helpers in this situation, even if their application cannot be explicitly applied.

The first is to notice that, in each of the Scriptures noted above and others, God does not attach conditions to the image-bearing aspect of His nature for men or women. In others words, He does not imply that men are given the responsibility of headship *only when they prove to be capable heads.* This "headship" is conferred on men as an aspect of *their* image bearing. He does not "become" the head of the home. He *is* the head of the home. This headship for men, like "helper" for women, is an aspect of their personhood. Their disposition. It is our responsibility to *help them lead* (hedge protect, empathize, lift and promote) regardless of their capability.

Secondly, the issue of "cannot" (because of maturity) is different from the refusal to lead. A husband who is a believer but refuses to lead his family *may be* subject to discipline, as this is a sign of habitual sin. At the very least, if this is the situation in your home, being a helper/promoter (wanting to advance

166 *Biblical Foundations for Manhood and Womanhood*, p. 89

the purpose and plan of God for your husband!) may mean a conversation that communicates your *desire* to submit to his headship but your concern that he doesn't seem to embrace his responsibility to lead. If he refuses, or rebuffs your concern, consider a response like: "I love you too much to allow you to abdicate this responsibility. I want us to go together to ask the church for help, but if you refuse to go with me I need you to know that I am going to go anyway." Then go!

Third, if you are married to a Christian who is less spiritually mature than you, here are just a few proactive ideas to consider:

Prayerfully identify a couple whose marriage is one that exemplifies God's plan for headship and helper. As you are able, do what you can to foster a friendship with them and talk with your husband about what you see in their marriage and family that you appreciate. Ask the Lord to open your husband's eyes to those aspects of spiritual leadership that are lacking in your family and encourage him to ask the other husband to "mentor" or disciple him in this area.

Encourage opportunities for your husband to step up and take responsibility in your home for the spiritual care of your family. *Resist the temptation to take over*. Remember my story on the very first few pages of this book? I became the "spiritual leader" because I had all the training and the years of experience, but I am sure (in hindsight) that our family would have been better served by Chas' leadership. God is sufficient to fill the gaps of your husband's leadership. It is *likely* that, as he begins to lead, *he will grow.* This is *clearly* the plan of God for your husband. Encourage him to lead, even if it feels "costly" for you. As he makes an effort, even if it's "baby steps," God will be faithful to bless and multiply that effort.

Finally, if you are married to a man who is not a believer, you are in a particularly difficult situation – but not one without hope! Peter makes the case in his first epistle that God *often uses the ezer/helper* woman to draw a man to himself! "*Be subject to your own husbands, so that even if some do not obey the word, they may be won without a word by the conduct of their wives, when they see your respectful and pure conduct*". That is a sobering and yet wonderful opportunity. You have the platform to point your husband to Jesus *without a word.* How? By *becoming Eve.* As you are transformed from being a woman who is self-promoting, self-protecting and self-absorbed into one who is *like Christ*, your husband – by the power of the Holy Spirit – may see your good works and glorify your Father who is in heaven. Amen?

A Note to Single Women

Sister, if you are single and you are waiting for God's man to become the spiritual leader of your home, may I just encourage you to thoughtfully consider all that has been said to your married sisters? As you do, keep these two things in mind:

Do not become impatient with the plan of God for your life and marry a man who does not love Jesus and love the church. I know *all* of the reasons this happens, and I understand the fear and the angst – and the glory of being loved. I would urge you not to allow the intoxication of emotion to overwhelm you and influence your godly womanhood. To do so, to marry a man who is not a Christian, is to *disobey the Lord*[167] and to risk your future as a family together. At the very least, I can promise you that there will be serious challenges to your marriage, and to your personal walk with God. Can these be overcome through the power of the Gospel? Indeed. But make no assumptions that they will. It is not a good start.

167 This admonition is very clear in 2 Corinthians 6:14. "Do not be unequally yoked with unbelievers."

Secondly, please do not subscribe to the fallacy that there is a "perfect Godly man" for you, one who checks all the boxes on your list of expectations. Do you want to marry a man who is a leader? Yes. Do you want to marry a man who is responsible? Yes. Do you want to marry a man who knows the Word? Yes. And the list goes on. I have seen "lists" that would disqualify even the Apostle Paul! You want to ask the Lord to give you a husband who *wants to be all of those things*. He ought to demonstrate a *desire* and a *commitment* to grow into the man that God means for him to be. Give him time and focus on your own *becoming*! You will be pleasantly encouraged over the years as that list begins to fade in your memory and the man that you married matures into the godly man that you had hoped for!

Putting It All Together

HELP. God displayed His *ezer* character and nature in His relationship to Rahab and she, in turn, was *being transformed* as she sought to become like Him in the context of her family and *all who belonged to her*. Rahab's story is replayed over and over throughout the generations as God proves His *helper* affection for women – hedge protecting, empathizing, lifting and promoting.

Every family is unique, and each woman of God will make application of the theology of biblical womanhood in her home according to her own circumstance. Whether you are a single mom raising children on your own, a wife married to a man who is not yet walking with the Lord, a woman married to a godly man who leads your family and supports you, or a single woman who has yet to marry and have a family of your own, these principles apply to your *becoming Eve*.

If we are to recover the *ezer* identity of the woman that God created in the Garden, we will take all of these things and "ponder them in our hearts" before the Lord. Resist the temptation to begin making a list of things to *do*. Instead, just sit quietly, for several days or weeks, and reflect on who you are in your soul before the Lord as it relates to *all who belong to you*. What does it mean to *become Eve* here?

Are you anxious to protect them, to be a shield and defender, against the chaos, stress, and pressure – the tribulation – in the world?

Are you willing to enter into their circumstance either by remembering your own history and experience or seeking to understand what you do not yet know?

Are you engaged in the effort to sustain their vitality? Are you able to take them to God's Word to lift them out of despair, discouragement and fear?

Are you interested in *who they are becoming*? Encouraging and equipping them in their strengths and weaknesses?

Most importantly, do you see God doing these things for you? Remember where we began this chapter? Being a "royal" has its perks. You are a "royal." A daughter of your *ezer* King. All of the benefits that we have ascribed to *all who belong to you* are yours in Christ. He is your Hedge protector. Your Empathizer. Your Lifter. Your Promoter.

As you live in light of your royal privilege, what might God do in the lives of *all who belong to you*?

A Footnote for Wives Who Live With Difficult Husbands

Without fail, when I teach this material to a group of women – whether there are ten or 200 – someone comes to me and says, "Are you saying I should live this way with my husband *no matter what*? That I ought to protect him, empathize with him, encourage him, and promote him at my own expense *even if he treats me like a doormat* (or worse)?"

This is a difficult issue to address in general, on paper. My immediate response is *always*, "If you are married to man who consistently does not love you as Christ loved the church – if he is rude, dismissive, angry, withholding, threatening, demanding, etc. – to you or to your children, you absolutely *must* tell an elder or pastor." That admonition is true whether the husband is a church member or not, a Christian or not, an elder, deacon or pastor. The bottom line is that to live passively in such a way with anyone is not *helping*.

When we talk about being a helper/*hedge protector*, sometimes that means protecting people from the consequences of their own sin by *not* maintaining status quo. It may require careful confrontation.

Empathizing with a person who has a destructive pattern of sin in his life means seeking to understand, but remember that we don't seek understanding as an end in itself. We seek to understand *so that we can help.*

Exercising our ezer/*lifter disposition* means that we are inclined to pull the one that we love *out of the pit* – not get down in the pit *with him.*

Finally, *promoting* the purposes and plans of God in the life of a loved one who habitually sins against us, and against others, means *not dismissing* his sin. It is *clearly* not God's plan for his life that he live comfortably in his sin. (Note: It is also not God's plan for your sanctification that you submit yourself to repeated acts of sin against you.)

In his second epistle to the church at Corinth, Paul makes reference to a letter that is not included in Scripture. It was, apparently, a stinging letter of rebuke to the church for some failure that threatened its effective ministry. The letter was so harsh that it caused the church to *grieve* and *repent.* This is Paul's response:

"Even if I made you grieve with my letter, I do not regret it ... I rejoice, not because you were grieved, but because you were ***grieved into repenting.*** *For you felt a godly grief, so that you suffered no loss through us. For godly grief produces repentance that leads to salvation without regret."*[168]

This is the ultimate *helper mentality.* That, in circumstances like those described above, we long for the one that we love to be "grieved into repenting." Toward that end, we must ask the Lord to give clarity, confidence and courage so that we are able to do whatever it takes to *become Eve.* Typically, that requires, at the very least, exposing the pattern of sin to someone with authority who can intervene. A leader at the church is the most appropriate advocate in most situations.

This is hard and it is risky. I do not offer this word of admonition without understanding the potential cost to you. But, sister, remember two things:

Ultimately the purpose of God for your life is that you would be *transformed into the image of Christ* who *made Himself nothing* on your behalf. It was a great sacrifice of His own comfort and security. This is our pattern for life.

Who is **your Ezer**? What do you know is true about God? *Remember Sarah's story.* God will **never fail you.** Never. Be obedient. Be faithful. Be humbly courageous.

Be a Helper.

168 2 Corinthians 7:8-10

Chapter Ten

THE HELPER TABERNACLE

There's a little-known of period in our nation's history that's referred to as the "Baby Scoop" era. It started after the end of World War II and ended in the early '70s. These years experienced an increased rate of premarital pregnancies and subsequently, a higher rate of newborn adoptions.

From a pro-life perspective, there were many good things about this. However, unbeknown to friends and all but close family, many girls who became pregnant were secreted away, often to "maternity homes" characterized as "prison for pregnant girls." They were shamed. Belittled. Shunned. Afraid.

More often than not, these young mothers, presented with no other option, were coerced into "adopting away" their newborn babies. Those who resisted found themselves faced with fees that had to be paid in full before their babies could be released to them. In effect, the babies were "held for ransom" until the mother, typically unable to meet the required financial demands, gave in. The trauma endured by these women is only recently being revealed.

While their suffering is unimaginable to most of us, it pales in comparison to the fate that awaited Mary, when it was discovered that she was pregnant before she and Joseph were married. Her pregnancy placed her at considerable risk, in a country and community that were decidedly *against* having babies out of wedlock. At best, Mary's family might allow her to continue to live at home, but her presumed adultery would no doubt compromise their standing in the community. Joseph would probably reject her and, if he did, no upstanding man would ever marry her. The stigma of her "situation" would always remain with her. At worst, Mary could have been stoned. The Old Testament law, according to Deuteronomy 22,[169] provided for this, and stoning for adultery still took place in Mary's generation, in first-century Palestine.[170]

She had nowhere to go. She couldn't go to the city and be lost in its anonymity. There were no "maternity homes." This was a family-centered culture where a woman's work and worth revolved around home and family. There was no place for a single woman, particularly one who had been soiled, except perhaps as a prostitute.

From a purely human perspective, Mary's prospects were grim. She had heartily and humbly agreed with the Lord when visited by the angel, declaring her allegiance to His plan: *"Behold, I am the servant of the Lord; let it be to me according to your Word."*[171] But now the cost of her decision was painfully apparent.

Scripture does not give us any information about how Mary's family responded to her impending motherhood. We do not know if they believed her account of the Angel's message. We do not know if they told their friends and neighbors, or if they tried to keep Mary out of sight. We also have no clue about Mary's girl friends. She was probably only about fourteen. Can you imagine what they must have said? Even without a hint in the Word about Mary's "support system," it is not a stretch to imagine that this was a challenging and perhaps lonely circumstance for the young mother-to-be.

But sometime during her maternity season, Mary made a

169 Deuteronomy 22:20, 21
170 *ESV Study Bible* Notes, Matthew 1:19
171 Luke 1:38

trip to visit her cousin Elizabeth who was also "with child." We know that Elizabeth was a great deal older than Mary, since Luke describes her as being (with her husband) *"advanced in years."* [172] Elizabeth's pregnancy was no less miraculous than Mary's![173] So Mary went to the home of Zechariah and Elizabeth, staying with them for about three months.

Elizabeth

It is easy to imagine that Mary had a lot of questions, both practical and spiritual, as she puzzled over God's plan for her life. She must have felt both excited and afraid at the prospect of this impending motherhood, full of enthusiasm, yet aware of the many challenges ahead. Would her friends still be her friends? Would people ever stop talking about her? Would Joseph really love her? Would she be a good mother? A good wife?

So God gave Mary her *ezer*-cousin, Elizabeth. Elizabeth would provide a quiet and restful home for Mary to think, talk, and ask questions. She would share Mary's enthusiasm and join her in all the experiences of pregnancy. Elizabeth and Zechariah had been married for many years, but she would remember what it was like to be young and in love. To wonder about married life. Can't you picture the two expectant cousins taking long walks, sitting up late into the night, so that Mary could talk and Elizabeth listen?

Elizabeth had her own story of God's steadfast love and faithfulness throughout all the seasons and situations of her life. Luke describes the older woman as "righteous ... walking blamelessly in all the commandments and statutes of the Lord," and "filled with the Holy Spirit," which suggests that she was a wise,

172 Luke 1:7
173 See her story, Luke 1

thoughtful woman of the Word. As Mary shared her fears and concerns and expectations, God would use Elizabeth to lift her countenance and to correct her childish thinking when it was necessary. She would have given Mary Scripture to hang onto so that her perspective was rooted not in her own youth or even her unique spiritual experience, but in God's Word. Perhaps out of her own story, she was able to help Mary trust God's promises even when she was discouraged or afraid.

One of the greatest gifts given to Mary in these early days of her pregnancy was the blessing that Elizabeth pronounced when Mary arrived on her doorstep. "And why is this granted to me that the mother of my Lord should come to me? For behold, when the sound of your greeting came to my ears, the baby in my womb leaped for joy. And blessed is she who believed that there would be a fulfillment of what was spoken to her from the Lord." This sentiment, this great anticipation that Elizabeth had for Mary's life as the mother of the Savior, must have resonated throughout the days and weeks that followed. When Mary returned home after three months, she would have been confident in her resolve to honor God's plan and purpose for her and for Joseph – at least in part because of Elizabeth's boldly prophetic assurance!

Mary was helped by her *ezer*-cousin, Elizabeth. The older woman was a hedge of protection for the younger. Elizabeth *empathized* with Mary, *lifted* and *promoted* the plans and purposes of God for her. Isn't that a great illustration of *becoming Eve?*

I want to be just like Elizabeth! This is a beautiful and strategic picture of what it means to have the disposition of a godly woman, an *ezer*, in the context of the church. As we explore this very important aspect of our unique image-bearing opportunity, we have two categories for consideration.

The first is our relationships to other women in the church, like Elizabeth and Mary. Paul admonished pastor Titus to encourage *"older women to teach what is good, and so train the young women to love their husbands and children, to be self-controlled, pure, working at home, kind, submissive to their own husbands, that the word of God may not be reviled."*[174]

We could draw many applications just from that admonition, but we are not limited to this verse in Titus as we consider our being transformed into the *ezer* image of God. We will see this dynamic unfold throughout the New Testament as we consider our relationships to our sisters in the church.

Secondly, we want to look carefully at God's plan for His daughters in the context of our relationships with the men in our churches. This will not be an exposition of what men can do and women cannot. Remember that our thinking about godly womanhood is more about *who we are becoming* than about what we can and/or cannot **do**.

However, there is a foundational truth that will undergird our consideration of this subject. The principle of headship in the church is set forth clearly in the Scripture in texts such as 1 Timothy 2:11-14. Here Paul affirms the image-bearing differences that God designed at the time of creation between man and woman. In the church as in the home, one of those differences works itself out in the primary responsibility for leadership and authoritative teaching (preaching) being held by men. Very simply, and in general, I would commend this summary statement by professor and author George Knight:

"There are two basic Biblical truths relating to men and

174 Titus 2:2-5

women that must be affirmed and upheld in the life of the church. The first is their equality as bearers of God's image and as fellow Christians. The second is the leadership role to which men are called by God in the church so that by apostolic injunction based on God's creative action women are not allowed to 'teach or exercise authority over a man.'"[175]

It is from this vantage point that we will dig into this potentially challenging topic.

Body, Building, and Bride

It seems prudent here to define what we mean when we make reference to "the church." There is a current trend among evangelicals to embrace the idea that a *personal* relationship with Jesus is singularly important to such an extent that church affiliation is unnecessary and, in some cases, may be an actual hindrance to personal spiritual growth.[176] A full response to such thinking is not possible here, but it must be addressed briefly because our ability to be transformed into the *ezer* image of God depends on a biblical understanding of church membership and participation.

Be assured: a personal response to the Gospel, repentance and a subsequent commitment to faith in Jesus Christ as Savior is necessary for salvation. Paul makes this point repeatedly with verses like: *"If* you *[personal pronoun] confess with your mouth that Jesus is Lord and believe in your heart that God raised Him from the dead, you will be saved."*[177] Every person who would desire to be saved from her own sin and from eternal death *must* come to

175 George Knight, "The Family & The Church," *Recovering Biblical Manhood & Womanhood*, p. 351
176 *You Lost Me: Why Young Christians are leaving the Church and Rethinking Faith*, David Kinnaman, p. 11
177 Romans 10:9

faith in Christ as an individual.

That said, Scripture consistently affirms that genuine faith expresses itself in the context of a local body of Christians called "the church." The modern "Jesus-and-me" faith is misinformed at best and harmful at worst. Throughout his oft-repeated treatise on marriage in Ephesians 5, Paul makes reference to Christ's love for "the church." Six times in eleven verses, the Apostle refers to Christ and "the church" as the object lesson for husbands who would seek to love their wives. He speaks of Christ's love for the church, His sanctifying of the church, His nourishing and cherishing the church. Perhaps the strongest application of this covenant between Christ and the church is Paul's statement in verse 25: *"Husbands, love your wives, as Christ loved the church and* ***gave himself up for her.****"* We cannot take away from the significance of Christ's death on the cross for individual sinners, but Paul clearly states here that Christ died **for the church**. Why, then, are we so quick to dismiss our affiliation with her and so loathe to nurture an affection for her?

Various texts throughout the Old and New Testament describe the church alternately as a Building,[178] a Body[179] and a Bride.[180] Each of these metaphors is *rich* with theology and deserving of pages and pages of attention. May I simply urge you to carefully dig into the Word on your own? You will quickly discover the beauty and poignant correlation of each of these illustrations in the Spirit's teaching about the church. These texts, particularly as they are considered *together*, offer a valuable theology of the church that will inform your perspective and challenge your thinking.

178 Ephesians 2:20-22
179 Romans 12:4, 5; Ephesians 4:16; 1 Corinthians 12:12-14
180 Ephesians 5:22-32

The Habit of Jesus

Consider Luke 4:16. Here, the Doctor makes a statement about the habit of Jesus that is easily missed in its context. *"Jesus went to Nazareth…on the Sabbath day he went to the synagogue* **as was His custom.**" Give that some thought. Jesus, who was the Son of God, went to church. Regularly.

Jesus went to church to hear the teaching of the Word (which seems a little unnecessary, since John 1 declares that Jesus *is The Word*). And yet He went. Week, after week, after week – habitually.

When He went to church, can't you imagine that He occasionally heard a less-than-inspiring sermon? What was His response? *He kept going to church.*

When He went to church, don't you think that sometimes the people around Him were unfriendly, rude even? What was His response? *He kept going to church.*

Do you think He always appreciated the way that the priest led the singing? Or the reading of the Word? Or the prayers? What was His response? *He kept going to church.*

What is interesting about each of those typical complaints about the church is that if anyone had a *right* to complain, it would have been Jesus. These people were reading, singing, hearing, reciting HIS WORD. Even when they disappointed Him, *He kept going.* Incredible.

It was Jesus' habit to maintain an affiliation with a local church. Jesus, the Son of God!

The Instruction of the Apostles

As we read the Pastoral Epistles, we find another note on the theology of church. Throughout the New Testament numerous passages indicate what we might consider official identification with a body of believers. There are commands of Scripture that cannot be put into practice without a direct, committed involvement in a local gathering of Christians. In particular, these texts address issues of *leaders* and *followers*.

The Apostles speak repeatedly to "elders" and "overseers" about the care of the "flock" in verses such as 1 Peter 1:3, which speaks of the *"flock under your care."* 1 and 2 Timothy speak to the *"elders of the church"* and *"elders* among *you"* seven times. Hebrews 13:7 urges readers to *"obey leaders and submit to those who **keep watch over you.**"* James 5:14 gives instruction to elders regarding the anointing of those who were sick *among them* (that is, the local Body).

Each of these admonitions and many others can only be reasonably applied if the people whom the writer addresses have a specific and identifiable "flock" under their care. It simply does not make sense that Peter would urge the leaders to care for the flock with the expectation that "the flock" included any sheep that just happened to be in the area!

In *The Enduring Community*, Brian Habig and Les Newsom make what will be a fitting concluding statement on the issue of church affiliation for God's people:

"The most faithful representation of the history of the Bible sees the church's origin in the mind of God before the foundations of the Earth. God, in love, was making people in His image ... fundamentally, people were to be in fellowship."[181]

I suspect you may be wondering "What does this have to do with being a *helper*?" We need to be convinced of two things: First, that we bring something to the ecclesiastical table that is of eternal value *as women* and second, that the church is *imperative* for our *ezer*-image-bearing walk with God. It has been said

181 *The Enduring Community*, p. 67

that "the church is just one generation away from extinction" and I understand the sentiment behind that statement. But Scripture assures us that the church will *never* "disappear," at least not until Jesus comes. Jesus promised Peter, *"Upon this rock I will build my church, and the gates of hell will not prevail against it."*[182] The church is secure.

But I am beginning to wonder what it will look like in five years. Ten years. Twenty years. What will my grandson's church be like? This is a serious and sober time. *All* believers need to be alert and fully informed about our Biblical responsibility to the church. But *women* believers have a strategic opportunity as we exercise our *ezer* disposition in the context of this beloved body, the church. Let's get on with it!

For the Love of Women in the Church

"Our soul waits for the Lord for He is our ezer and our shield."

It will come as no surprise to you that there are very real pressures and fears faced by women in the church. Every church has its own version of these challenges, but they present themselves almost universally, if there are women around.

- The pressure to have perfect marriages and perfect children.
- The pressure to "have it together."
- The fear of failure.
- The fear of being different.

This little sampling ought to spur your thinking about your own church. What are women afraid of? What causes them to withdraw, stay on the "fringe", refuse to take on leadership positions? What fuels the fires of exclusivity and pride?

182 Matthew 16:18

Whatever the answers to those questions relative to your church, being transformed into the image of Christ and growing in your *ezer* disposition means that you want to help the church to be a safe place, and you want to be a safe person for the people in your little circle of influence. As you engage with the women around you, your *helper*/hedge-protector disposition expresses itself in the freedom for women to ask hard questions, express frustration, disappointment and even anger without fear of rebuke or dismissal. Remember Jesus and Martha? She was impertinent and out of line. But Jesus was more concerned with her soul than with her manners. This is the *ezer* disposition in the church.

A *helper*/hedge-protector understands and applies the difference between "preference" and "principle." So her friends may choose to make choices about schooling for their children, working outside the home, bottle or breast feeding, cloth diapers or disposable, etc., etc., etc., without fear of her judgment.

One aspect of being a *hedge protector* for our sisters in the church is the commitment to depend on Scripture as the source for our counsel and care. Often, the books and blogs that are widely read, quoted, and assimilated into our conversations offer "truth" that is extra-biblical, or unbiblical. Our own opinions or ideas may be good, but we have seen repeatedly the value of God's Word as our basis for helping. FBI experts tell us that the only sure way to spot a counterfeit bill of currency is to be intimately and expertly familiar with "the real thing." *Becoming Eve* requires no less. Our sisters will suffer from the counterfeit faith that seeps into our helping theology if we are not dependent on Scripture as our "*only rule of faith and practice.*"

The disposition of *ezer*-hedge-protector is also revealed in the setting of her disappointment, or the disappointment of others in the church. Even in the "best" church, it is only a matter of time before something happens that causes the godly woman to be distressed. Her choices in this season are a reflection of her disposition. How will she protect the "*peace and purity of the church*"? She has Matthew 18 in mind as she thoughtfully chooses when to speak and what to say and when to choose prayerful silence. The unity of the church, Jesus' passionate priority, is her *ezer–hedge protecting* goal.

"O Lord, you have helped me and comforted me."

I was standing in line at a local coffee shop recently when I overheard a conversation between two women who were behind me.

"She's acting like a teenager. It's embarrassing."

"Well, she's excited."

"I'm aware. But really, all of this hullabaloo about a wedding at her age!"

"I know. You would think at 50-something they would have the sense to just go to an island and have a ceremony."

"An island? I think they should just go to the courthouse. And the shower? Who has a shower for a 50-year old bride? What could she possibly need that she doesn't already have?"

Okay, granted. I don't know the whole story. But I wanted to turn around and say, "Really? Don't you remember what it was like to be in love? Weren't you so excited when you were first engaged that you wanted everyone to know it, and to be included? Is that any less true for people over 50 than for teenagers?" Sigh.

Unfortunately, some version of this scene plays out with regularity among women at church. Instead of expressing the heart of Christ as an *ezer/empathizer*, we are quick to judge. Because we are each in different seasons and situations, and we each have our own story, we tend to be critical of others – assuming their motivation, perhaps harboring our own bitterness and hurt, and not taking the time to remember. We have acknowledged the generational challenges that we face at church, but generational differences are not the only issues that threaten to divide us. Marital status. Spiritual maturity. Family choices. Financial challenges. Employment status. If women are not being transformed into the image of God in Christ, we will erect so many walls that our churches will be chopped up into tiny little cubicles of isolation.

Instead, my *ezer/empathizer* disposition allows me to remember what it was like to be single. To be a new Christian. To have a new baby. To be a newlywed. To be financially strapped. To have a demanding job. Rather than seeing things through my own eyes, I am able to step outside of my current circumstance and remember God's amazing grace and favor to me over the years. I *remember* so that I can comfort and encourage my sister with the comfort that I received.[183]

And when *remembering* is not helpful, an *ezer/empathizer* seeks to understand. *Becoming Eve* means that we want to be strategically engaged with people, so that our time together is fruitful. Toward that end, it is helpful to think proactively for conversations, planning for two or three very specific questions to draw out someone's story. Remember Proverbs 20:5, "*The purpose in a man's heart is like deep water, but a man*

183 1 Corinthians 1:4

of understanding will draw it out." Once she starts talking, the *ezer/empathizer* listens!

Another helpful approach to seek to understand is to physically enter her world. One of our young moms has three children under the age of three (yes, it's possible). I went to her house to visit and brought her a vanilla latte. I spent more time playing with the children and snuggling the baby than chatting with the mama, but it was an eye-opening experience and one that helped me to understand why she *never got her Bible study done!*

"May He send you ezer from the sanctuary and grant you support from Zion."

The idea of being an *ezer/lifter* is applicable both as we cultivate a culture of vitality and health (breathe life!) and as we persevere, like Jeremiah's friends, with people who are weary, discouraged or without hope, helping to lift them out of the cistern of despair. We've already covered some of this ground, for a church that is characterized as a safe place and one where people are empathetic, understanding and full of grace may be a healthy, dynamic and thriving church.

Or it may be the seemingly spiritual version of a support group. Which is not a criticism of support groups, but the church must be more than a comfortable, safe and accepting spiritual home. One predominant aspect of vitality for the church is its commitment to Truth, the preaching, teaching and discipline of the Word. Since we've already made the point that Scripture does not allow for a woman to preach, how are we to *become Eve* relative to a vigorous dedication to the Truth?

There are several applications of the helper/lifter that merit our consideration. The first is our willingness to *speak truth* to one another, cultivating relationships that are marked by intentional movement toward Christ and His transforming power. When one person lives in perpetual sin, and another relates passively towards her, neither woman is experiencing the lifting power of the Gospel.

Becoming Eve means that we risk having an awkward conversation for the redemptive benefit of restoring a wandering sister to healthy fellowship in the church.[184]

Assimilating truth is another aspect of *ezer*/lifter relationships that must be part of our church life together. A woman who is *becoming Eve* seeks to help by lifting her sister out of whichever pit is most threatening and *using Scripture to do so.* We've alluded to this from a "protective" perspective. But the deployment of God's promises is also our best means to encourage one another, to provide hope and vision.

Consider Psalm 125.

"I lift up my eyes to the hills. Where does my help come from? My help comes from the Lord, the maker of heaven and earth. He will not let your foot slip; He who keeps you will not stumble. The Lord is your keeper; The Lord is your shade by your right hand."

I lift up my eyes to the hills. Always the hills. It seems that I just get over one hill and, when I look up, another looms in front of me. Isn't that the experience of most of us? What will we do? How will we defeat despair and hopelessness? How will we gain the courage and tenacity to tackle the next hill?

Sitting with a woman who is fearful, discouraged, disap-

184 James 5:19, 20

pointed or simply weary, it is tempting to offer my own "words of wisdom" to try to urge her over that looming mountain. Sometimes that is helpful, and we've already suggested that our own experience of God ought to inform our ability to empathize with others. However, what this woman really needs is Truth, the sufficiency of the Word to cling to when her own perspective is biased by her circumstances. How will she stumble over that hill? By trusting the One who created the hills! The Lord will not let her foot slip. It is His Word that instructs her heart and mind and it is His Word that will inform her spirit, helping her to press on. This is *ezer-lifting* at its finest!

"I have granted ezer to one who is mighty; I have exalted one chosen from the people."

One of the spiritually healthiest and most winsome communities of adults at our church is our Senior Adults group. As one might expect, many of their members are actually struggling with very difficult health issues and some number of them will go to be with Jesus this year. But from the perspective of how you measure the vigor of "community," this group of close to 200 men and women demonstrates the kind of care, affection, camaraderie, commitment and support that is enviable to those of us who are not yet in their life stage. They really are a family.

Interestingly, when we have conversations with the gifted, sage, clever and often witty women from this community, they often remark that they "have nothing to offer" or that they are too "old and out of touch" to be of any help to the younger generation. Oh my. Nothing could be further from the truth and it is into these kind of conversations that *be-*

coming Eve as a promoter is perhaps most needful.

The desire to become a woman who helps other women in the church to discover and pursue the plans and purposes of God for their lives is a defining characteristic of *ezer* womanhood. This is the means to fully experience Paul's admonition to the church as a "body." Romans 12 describes this analogy: *"For as in one body we have many members, and the members do not all have the same function, so we, though many, are one body in Christ, and individually members one of another."* He goes on in this chapter and in 1 Corinthians 12 to elaborate on the importance of every part of the body understanding and embracing its function. *Becoming Eve* means that we partner with the Spirit to try to help our sisters discover their "function"!

As we think about being an *ezer/promoter* in the Body, it may be helpful to think about some common barriers that keep women from living up to their potential in Christ.

It may be difficult for a woman to see and aspire to the plans and purposes of God for her life because of the fear and insecurity that informs her story. Many women (the statistics are staggering) have endured troubled family dynamics,[185] and these range on the scale from disappointing to horrific. Our ability and desire to engage with women as they navigate whatever means necessary to experience God's healing power and restorative grace is absolutely imperative as we seek to *become Eve* in the context of our church family. Often this will require pastoral and/or professional insight, but perhaps the most powerful influence *long term* in pro-

185 Included in the issue of helping women deal with traumatic history is the need to be sensitive to the failure of "the church" either to help her in the past or as a completely separate issue. In other words, some women are paralyzed not by traumatic family history, but by some hurtful or painful experience of "church."

moting the purpose of God for a woman who has a traumatic history is the persistent friendship of a godly woman.

Another barrier may be a sister's limited exposure to Bible study and or church life in any form. She may not see God's purpose for her life because she is lost just trying to navigate Sunday School, worship, small groups, Bible study, nursery duty, the sacraments, and holiday rituals. You see the challenge. The regular routine related to church that is second-nature to most of us may have this new sister completely overwhelmed. An *ezer* promoter will look for ways to help her to gain confidence and competency and a love for the church!

Every woman in the church, from eighteen to eighty, is a part of the Body and each has the potential to be used by God for His own glory. Sometimes, His purposes are grand and big and far-reaching. More often than not, His plans and purposes for our lives are discovered as we quietly encourage one another, helping each other to exercise our giftedness, challenge one another's weaknesses and fill in the gaps of our shortcomings. This is the beauty of sisterhood in the Body.

The godly woman who is *becoming Eve* has a deep and sincere commitment to protecting, empathizing, lifting and promoting her sisters at church. She sees her own life through the lens of the grace and mercy she has received at the hand of *ezer*-God and she longs to bear His image in her relationships and ministry opportunities with the women who worship and serve with her. She is fiercely committed to the church and deeply invested in its people. Among her sisters, this woman is a life-giver.

For the Love of the Brothers in the Church

"Our soul waits for the Lord for He is our ezer and our shield."

Which brings us to the issue of *becoming Eve,* being transformed into the *ezer* image of God as that disposition affects our brothers in the church. What does it mean to be a *hedge protector* in these relationships? It is likely that our interaction with the men who are leaders in the church is more removed, less frequent, than our association with women so hedge protecting has a different application here. Our *hedge-protecting* disposition may express itself more in how we *think* about them and how we talk about them than in actual, personal contact. Consider these strategic questions:

- Is there an expectation that they never fail? Never make a wrong decision?

- Is their reputation safe with you? Are you reluctant to participate in conversation about any one of them in particular, or the leadership in general, that is negative and/or destructive?

- Are you anxious to protect their marriages, so that you are thoughtful about what you wear and how you carry yourself?

- When invited, do you have the posture of one who wants to *help* or one who wants to *fix*?

These men, as spiritual leaders in the church, are strategically positioned for attack from the enemy. They should have nothing to fear from a woman who is *becoming Eve*. Our *ezer-hedge protector* disposition should overflow in our prayer for the leaders and their families, our charitable conversation about them to others and our effort to protect them from unnecessary burden. We want to grow in our ability to allow these men the freedom to be less than perfect, and we want to extend the grace and charity to *always believe the best* about them!

"O Lord, you have helped me and comforted me."

Remember the Harper Lee quote from *To Kill a Mockingbird*? "You never really understand a person until you consider things from his point of view...until you climb into his skin and walk around in it." That advice is so powerful as we think about empathy with our brothers at church. Far from comprehensive, think about the "point of view" of our brothers:

- How much criticism do they receive for every decision they make?
- How much unsolicited input do they receive before making a decision?
- Who listens when they are struggling, or disappointed, or angry or hurt?
- How many hours of sleep do they lose because of meetings, teaching preparation, shepherding cases, administrative work?

The effort to seek understanding is particularly important as the ezer/empathizer grows in her appreciation of and affection for the spiritual leaders in her church. It will require determination to cultivate this environment of understanding, partly because of the unique differences between men and women but also because women are often somewhat removed from the decision-making process at church. Whether or not the godly woman agrees with that structure is not as much at issue as how she responds to it.

Without the discipline of seeking to understand, a chasm of disappointment and bitterness may threaten the church family. Even in the best circumstances, the decisions and actions of church leaders can be misinterpreted or misunderstood and the disposition of the ezer/helper must always be to bring understanding if at all possible. The tone of the *ezer*/ empathizer who is seeking understanding will always be quick to listen, slow to respond, slower still to manipulate, maneuver or control a conversation or circumstance. She will, instead, "walk around in his skin" a bit, just to see things from his point of view.

"May He send you ezer from the sanctuary and grant you support from Zion."

What does this mean for our men? Our spiritual leaders in the church? As I bear the *ezer*/lifter image of God as a strong support, always in my mind is the desire to breathe life into their ministry and families. This idea incorporates much of what we've already addressed, but perhaps one particular concern may be offered here.

I have the privilege of singing on our worship team. We rehearse every week on Wednesday evenings and again just before worship on Sunday. I love this ministry opportunity partly because I have tremendous respect and deep affection for our Worship Pastor. However, one evening during rehearsal he gave some direction or information that was, well, wrong. It was a minor detail and one that could have easily been corrected at another time, but in a moment of self-importance, I corrected him and it had the effect of "deflating" him. I could tell that it was the last straw on a very long day.

Sigh. My impertinence bugged me for several days until I finally had the opportunity to speak to him and personally ask his forgiveness. (Which, not surprisingly, he readily offered!)

We've already pointed out that our pastors, elders, deacons and other spiritual leaders in the church are on the receiving end of criticism, correction and reproach. In fact, *The New York Times* reported: "Members of the clergy now suffer from obesity, hypertension and depression at rates higher than most Americans. In the last decade, their use of antidepressants has risen, while their life expectancy has fallen. Many would change jobs if they could."[186] Statistics can be deceiving, and they are often conflicting depending on which organization is responsible for the survey or poll. But in this case, no matter which survey you cite, the statistics are heartbreaking.

- 33% of pastors surveyed report that being in ministry is an outright hazard to their family.
- Up to 1,500 pastors leave their ministry every month due to burnout, conflict or moral failure.
- 57% of pastors are so discouraged that they would leave the ministry if they could find another way to support their families

In his book *Pastors at Greater Risk*, H. B. London warns that the risks in ministry to pastors and their lay leaders are greater than ever. He suggests "this struggle takes a terrible toll, as pastors wrestle with crammed calendars, hectic homes, splintered dreams, starved intimacy and shriveled purpose. Some quit in utter hopelessness. Others lapse into passivity. And many of the rest just hold on by their fingernails."[187]

186 *The New York Times*, "Taking a Break from the Lord's Work," Paul Vitello, August 1, 2010
187 H. B. London, Jr. *Pastors at Greater Risk*, p. 14 and 15

What's an *ezer* to do? As a woman who is *becoming Eve*, just the reading of those few paragraphs causes me to pray fervently against such despair among my pastors and our elders. It is my desperate desire that their experience be different, that we, as their people, breathe life into them personally and into their families.

At the very least, returning to my story about John, this means that I steward my criticism carefully. Knowing that these men hear from plenty of other people about what they are doing "wrong," being an *ezer*/lifter inspires my heart and mind to look for good things to say, encouraging stories to tell, ways that I can lift up the sagging souls of my brothers so that they will not crumble under the pressure of life and ministry. I want to be a woman to whom they can look for support – an *ezer* who sustains and lifts up. Can I get an Amen?

"I have granted ezer to one who is mighty; I have exalted one chosen from the people."

The late Elisabeth Elliot, in a collection of short essays from her newsletter, cited this verse from 1 Chronicles 11:10 in relationship to her marriage: "These are the chiefs of David's mighty men, who gave him strong support and made him king." Elliot suggested that this posture of David's mighty men informed her perspective of her disposition in marriage. That it was her highest goal to do all that she could to make her husband king.

I would affirm her application (she was Elisabeth Elliot, after all!) and would, in fact, take it one step further. As I relate to our pastors, elders and diaconate this is my highest goal: that I would do all that I can to help them to be the very best leaders that they can be. Strategically that means…

I will prayerfully and intentionally think about the plans and purposes of God for their lives and do what I can to promote them asking myself literally, "How can I help?"

I will not capitalize on their weaknesses but will instead do everything I can to mitigate the impact any weaknesses may have on their ministry. This means that I will not mock them, in public or private, but I will show them the respect they deserve.

I will not undermine their authority but will, instead, submit cheerfully.

I will set aside my own agenda in favor of theirs.

As an *ezer*/promoter, I want to cultivate a relationship with my brothers that is marked by gracious submission, respect and confidence. That means, at least in part, that I promote the plans and decisions that the pastoral leadership sets forth, doing all that I can to help them succeed. My disposition to promote my own agenda, desires and/or giftedness is being transformed into the heart of God for His plans and purposes for others. The question is: how can I help?

Putting It All Together

HELP. God demonstrated His own *ezer* character and nature as He gave Elizabeth to Mary at a strategic season in that young woman's life. God used Elizabeth to help Mary feel safe and secure, to empathize with her and encourage her, to lift her heart and mind to the fullness of her faith and to help her to press on toward the high calling of God on her life!

The church needs women who, like Elizabeth, *breathe life*

by *helping*. It is, in part, our mission to protect, empathize, lift and promote our sisters and brothers in the church. We don't do this alone, but we do it uniquely. Without the commitment of *ezer*-women, the Bride of Christ will suffer. We have barely scratched the surface of what such commitment means, but the importance of the influence of godly women on the future of the church cannot be overstated.

As you ponder your desire to *be transformed* into the likeness of Christ, reflecting the *ezer* image of a helper in the church, what does it mean for you to *become Eve* here?

What does it mean to be a *shield* and *defender* against the pressure of perfection, exclusivity and uniformity in the church?

How are you able to *empathize* and *comfort* those who are in different seasons and situations in life and faith?

Are you engaged in sustaining the vitality of the church by clinging to the Truth? Are you a woman who *lifts up* the sagging souls of your brothers and sisters with words and actions that encourage and inspire hope?

Finally, are you looking for ways to *promote* the plans and purposes of God in the lives of the men and women in your church?

Most importantly, do you see God doing these things for you as you walk with Him in the context of Body life? Take a little personal inventory. Where do you need the *Helper* to breathe life into *your own soul* so that you might be transformed today?

Chapter Eleven

THE HELPER NEIGHBORHOOD

Sheryl Sandberg is the Chief Operating Officer at Facebook and its number two executive, after CEO Mark Zuckerberg. She's on *Fortune*'s list of the 50 Most Powerful Women in Business and *Time*'s list of the 100 Most Influential People in the World. Her book, *Lean in: Women, Work and the Will to Lead* spent 51 weeks on *The New York Times* Bestseller List.[188] She has helped build Facebook® into a multibillion-dollar company, and now she wants to build a new women's movement.

Ms. Sandberg's message can be summarized in a very simple but loaded proposition: A woman *can* have it all. Career. Husband. Children. Friendships. Her premise is that, while inequality clearly still characterizes the American workplace (women still earn just 77 cents for every $1 for a man[189]), many of the barriers to women's advancement are self-imposed. Her own rise to success is about her choice to be ambitious, bold, confident and aggressive. She is not always well regarded by either gender, but with a net worth of $1.7 billion, she has achieved a measure of success that few women in America will ever see.

Ms. Sandberg is, for many American women, a modern-day hero. Her book is widely regarded as this generation's manifesto on feminism[190], a title earned from some of its claims:

> "In the future, there will be no female leaders. There

188 As of March 2014
189 Institute for Women's Policy Research (quoted in USA Today article)
190 *USA Today,* March 11, 2013 "Facebook's Sandberg wants to lead new women's movement," Jon Swartz

> will be just leaders."
>
> "Real change will come when powerful women are less of an exception."
>
> "A truly equal world would be one where women ran half our countries and companies and men ran half our homes."
>
> "Aggressive and hard-charging women violate unwritten rules about acceptable social conduct. Men are continually applauded for being ambitious and powerful and successful, but women who display these same traits often pay a social penalty. Female accomplishments come at a cost."

Which prompts the question: What's a godly woman to do?

As Ms. Sandberg tackles the very real challenges that women face in the workplace, Christian women need to consider *ezer*-image bearing in the context of the world in which we live.

Is Sandberg's wisdom applicable to our experience? Are we to look to her as a role model? If so, how does the *helper* disposition apply? And, on the contrary, if Sheryl Sandberg's example and manifesto ought not be ours, then how do we know how to live as "successful" godly women in the world?

Angel of Mercy

Angelina Jolie is said to be Hollywood's highest-paid actress,[191] earning $33 million in 2013. Since her film career began in 1995, Jolie has starred in fifteen films and been nominated for and or/received the same number of awards. In 2015, a global survey found her to be the "most admired woman in the world."

191 Information on Angelina Jolie for this section from Wikipedia, "Angelina Jolie"

In addition to her screen presence, Jolie holds the position of Goodwill Ambassador for the United Nations High Commissioner for Refugees. She has traveled on more than fifty missions to dozens of countries where basic humanitarian needs are threatened. She has donated millions of dollars and launched numerous non-profit agencies to address the issues that concern her. Her biography on Wikipedia is impressive, with headings such as "Conservation and Community Development", "Child Immigration and Education" and "Human Rights and Women's Rights."

Most recently, Jolie has engendered the admiration and respect of women around the world for publicly sharing her cancer prevention surgeries. Her influence, called by *Time* magazine "the Angelina Effect," has resulted in a measured increase in gene testing among women in not only the United States, but in the UK, Canada, India and numerous other European countries.

To many, Angelina Jolie is the "Mother Teresa" of our generation. Hers is the face of mercy and hope for millions of people. Is she a role model for today's godly woman? What do we have to learn from Jolie's commitment to humanitarian efforts in the world? How does the *helper* disposition inform our thinking?

The Times They are A-Changin'

Bob Dylan, the poetic (if not always pleasant) voice of the Sixties, wrote these words that could describe what's happening for women in our world today:

> "Your old road is rapidly agin'
> Please get out of the new one
> If you can't lend your hand
> For the times they are a-changin'"[192]

192 Bob Dylan, "The Times They Are A-Changin"

The old road is rapidly aging for women. Had my grandmother been asked, she could never have predicted a day where women led multibillion-dollar companies and traveled as ambassadors to war-torn and poverty-ravaged countries to effect change.

And yet this is the new road for women. It is changing so fast that by the time you read these words, they will be somewhat obsolete. I don't know how you feel about that, but given the time to consider it, I alternate between being paralyzed by fear and wanting to run to the hills (wherever that is) and hide from "progress." Here's what keeps me from looking for the nearest escape route: God Never Changes.

We began this discussion, dozens of pages past, with three principles from God's Word that have been our foundation:

- God created all people, men and women, in His image.
- God created all people, men and women, *equal* in His image. Equal does not mean same.
- God created men and women to be different in ways that were designed for His glory and for our good at the time of creation.

These truths, while established before time began, are no less true *today* – in the world of Sheryl Sandberg and Angelina Jolie – than they were in the Garden of Eden when our first parents were fashioned by the hand of God.

The God, who was the *help* of Adam, and Abraham, and Moses, and Jacob, and Isaiah, and Mary, and Matthew, and Peter, and Lydia, and Paul…THIS GOD, their protector, their empathizer, their lifter and their promoter, THIS GOD HAS NOT CHANGED.

Times change.

Roles change.

Expectations change.

Relationships change.

Laws change.

GOD DOES NOT CHANGE. And His Word *does not change.*

We are tempted to believe that, because the landscape of our lives as women has shifted, *truth* has shifted. Morphed. Become more contemporary. More "relevant." As we begin to consider becoming Eve in the context of the world beyond home and church, we must acknowledge the immutability of God and His Word. He does not change. Truth does not change. What was true for Sarah (Mrs. Abraham) was true for my Grandmother. And for me. And for Sheryl Sandberg. And for Angelina Jolie. Whether or not these women acknowledge the Eternal Covenant-Keeping Creator God and His Word makes no difference to His character and Truth. These do not change with the "rapidly agin' road."

It follows, then, that the design of God for women to be *helpers,* created in His *ezer* image is true for every woman in every generation, regardless of her situation in life, her role, her season, or her circumstances. Perhaps it is more complicated today than ever before. But it is *no less true* or applicable.

How are we to live as godly women in a world where Sheryl Sandberg sets the bar of success and Angelina Jolie has broadened our horizons of mercy in the world? How does what we know to be *true* apply to the myriad challenges that confront women today? How might we grow in our deep love for God and our image-bearing of His *helper* nature?

"Come senators, congressmen
Please heed the call
Don't stand in the doorway
Don't block up the hall
For he that gets hurt
Will be he who has stalled
There's a battle outside ragin'
It'll soon shake your windows
And rattle your walls
For the times they are a-changin'"

Come, sister, and heed the call. There is a battle raging, but we have nothing to fear. Let's hang on to what we know is true and forge ahead in *faith*, knowing that our *Helper* goes before us and with Him, nothing is impossible!

The Wide Sphere of the World

Before charging ahead, however, we would do well to circumvent a landmine in the road. We have seen – in the context of both home and church – that it was God's design from the beginning of creation that the man would be the head of both his home and his church. Without specifically addressing submission, we have seen that the disposition of a *helper* in marriage and in the church has had the underlying foundation of the headship of husband and elder. We believe this to be a biblical expression of the goodness of God and a particular appropriation of His wisdom for men and women.

As we begin to broaden our vision for gender beyond home and church, particularly for godly womanhood, understanding what is clear and explicit in God's Word becomes somewhat challenging. God has chosen not to specifically address the thousands of occasions in which men and women interact in the business world, the community, in government and in education. While He has put a structure and order in place for husbands and wives, pastors and their churches, these same roles and expectations do not seem to apply as men and women relate in the world.

Headship and submission, in particular, do not apply to relationships between men and women beyond home and church. All of the texts in Scripture that give instruction to us on these issues are speaking to that limited context. Nowhere in God's Word are women called to submit universally to all men. Nor are men called universally to positions of authority over all women.

Landmine, huh?

Not really. While Scripture may not speak particularly to every *role* a woman might assume outside of her home and how she is to relate to every man, the *spirit* of God's plan for men and women to live and work together in ways that are consistent with His design is pervasive because it is rooted in our creation. Our image-bearing as men and women is not limited to husbands, wives, elders, pastors and church members. Our image-bearing is a part of our personhood; it therefore extends to every relationship in some form or fashion. While we are not called to *submit* to every man, we are to relate to them in a way that is consistent with our design!

Remember our three foundational principles, recalled already in this chapter? These principles are the framework for how we think about gender *in general* – in every context. God's plan to create us male and female in His image, equal but not the same, and with many differences is a perspective that is often called "complementarian" and it applies to all occasions of men and women doing life together. This is why it is so important to think about the application of *ezer* image-bearing as our disposition rather than our *role.*

In general, the idea is that when considered *together,* the inherent strengths and weaknesses of men (by the design of God at the time of creation) and the inherent strengths and weaknesses of women, are the perfect complement to each other. John Piper suggests "so that when life together is considered (and I don't just mean married life) the weaknesses of manhood are not weakness and the weaknesses of woman are not weakness. They are the complements that call forth different strengths in each other."[193] I love that vision for life.

I have a close friend who is single, in her thirties, independent and motivated in her career. She holds a position in upper management in her company and her employees are primarily men. It is a unique circumstance for a godly young woman. Over the years, we have had numerous conversations about this issue of *becoming Eve.* What does it mean to be a *helper* when you are the one in charge? One really significant lesson that Jill has learned is that it is possible to "affirm, receive and nurture the strength and leadership"[194] of the men who work for her without compromising her authority. I am regularly impressed and encouraged by Jill's mature womanhood as she looks for ways, *even as she leads them*, to honor the men who are in her employ.

So it's not a landmine. It is simply a speed bump that, taken carefully, ought not to derail us at all. Our world as women has expanded far beyond the "safe" confines of home and church. The times are changing, and we need to be prepared to respond in ways that are consistent with what we know is true from

193 *Recovering Biblical Manhood & Womanhood*, p. 40
194 John Piper's language, *Recovering Biblical Manhood & Womanhood,* in his definition of "The meaning of femininity," p. 41

God's Word. While we are not required to submit to the headship of every man, we must resist the temptation to make our own way, listen to the voice of the enemy and aggressively demand what is "rightfully ours." God's plan is good. This relational dynamic is possible for women who know and trust God who is our *helper*. We may live complementary lives with the men in our world because He is faithful and His plan is good.

The Boundaries of Our Dwelling Place (and Our Office, Our Gym, Our Library...)

What does it look like to be a godly woman in the workplace? How can a godly woman grow in her *ezer* disposition as she navigates work and home life? Is it possible, and biblical, to be a *helper* at home and a leader in the marketplace? How does your *becoming Eve* influence the parent's association, swim team or charity board? What are the eternal implications of biblical womanhood on the marginalized populations of your city? Is there an application of the *ezer* image of God that might change the world?

These issues represent the complexity of the godly woman's life. This is meant to encourage you to think deeply and pray passionately about godly womanhood *beyond* your Jerusalem, Judea and Samaria. As you do so, let's meander around the idea of bearing the *ezer* image of God "to the end of the earth" in our various spheres of influence outside of home and church.

Think about the numerous people, places and circumstances that make up your weekly routine. These might be neighbors, coworkers, tennis friends, play group moms, managers, work-out partners, or teachers. These are people whose lives intersect with yours on a fairly regular basis. Beyond these there are others – people you may not know, but with whom you have some contact: baristas, sales clerks, hair stylists, service people, police officers (hopefully not!). Does *ezer* image bearing have an impact on your interactions, even occasionally, with these people? Thinking even more broadly, how does your faith, and subsequent growing *helper* disposition, influence the city in which you live ... your country ... the world? Does that *really matter*?

It seems that it does. With regularity throughout Scripture, God strategically moves His people to particular places. *"Go from your country and your kindred and your father's house to the land that I will show you,"* [195] He instructed Abram. The Lord appeared to Isaac and said: *"Do not go down to Egypt; dwell in the land of which I shall tell you."*[196] The New Testament continues this idea that God has a plan for His people that includes where they will live and work and worship. Paul, in his famous sermon to the people in Athens, made this remark as evidence of God's sovereignty: *"And He made from one man every nation of mankind ... having determined allotted periods and the* ***boundaries of their dwelling place.****"* (Acts 17:26) Having formed the nations from one man, God then determined the *times* and *places* where each man (and woman) would live.

God, in His sovereignty, determines the boundaries of our dwelling place.[197]

God decides where we will live, and when we will live there. I suppose that's not rocket science, but how often we have given that any thought? God has determined where I will live in this season of my life. In which city. In which neighborhood. In which school district. On which street. In which house. The significance of that reality is sobering. Our understanding of

195 Genesis 12:1
196 Genesis 26:2
197 Acts 17:26

God's sovereign rule over every detail of our lives[198] informs our thinking here. I live in my home, in my neighborhood and city by God's design and for His purpose – which is ultimately His own glory. How is my *becoming Eve* significant in this context?

Scripture speaks to the influence of godliness among those who are in proximity to us. Texts like Isaiah 1:17 are clear: *"learn to do good; seek justice, correct oppression; bring justice to the fatherless, plead the widow's cause."* The writer of Hebrews admonishes his readers: *"Strive for peace with everyone, and for the holiness without which no one will see the Lord,"*[199] and *"Do not neglect to show hospitality to strangers ... remember those who are in prison, ... and those who are mistreated."*[200]

Clearly, God intends for our *living* to flow out of our faith so that the lives of others are drawn to the beauty and grace of the Gospel. The anticipation of such influence begins just a few feet from my home (or desk, or classroom). My life as a woman who loves Jesus has impact on those whom I see and interact with every day, but it does not stop there. The opportunity for God to draw people to Himself through the lives of godly women is not limited to these familiar relationships, but He uses His people in broader terms as we live and work and interact with and try to make a difference in our neighborhoods and cities as well.

This seems like an overwhelming expectation as I think about my community, the city in which I live and work. The needs seem so great, probably even greater than I know. Just a cursory look at the issues of justice and mercy are enough to discourage even the most passionate neighbor:

- 74,000 people in my community depend on food stamps

198 Romans 11:36 and Colossians 1:16
199 Hebrews 12:1
200 Hebrews 13:1-3

- More than 8,000 young people have dropped out of high school in the past year
- Since 1990, the number of incarcerated women has more than doubled in our city
- Our state consistently ranks in the top ten of the United States in the human trafficking industry

These are the people in my community. What can I possibly do to *help*?

WORLD Magazine proposes: "Individuals can help to transform lives one at a time, in a way that challenges recipients of help to take responsibility wherever they are, as they learn from God who they are." Further, I would suggest that in every age and every country and every season, **women** have been the individuals who have primarily championed mercy to the world. What comes to mind when you think about the following women?

- Clara Barton
- Florence Nightingale
- Mother Teresa
- Dorothea Dix

Isn't that intriguing? When we think about mercy, we typically think about women! It seems there has always been what has been called a "spring of mercy" in the female heart.[201]

Becoming Eve in the context of our community, our country, city, and neighborhood incorporates all of the aspects of *ezer* womanhood that we have considered to this point in ways that are perhaps a little more challenging to define. Nevertheless, the theology of the *ezer* disposition applies here. It must not be lost

201 *Female Piety*, John Angel James, 1854

on me that God has ordained the place in which I live, the office where I report daily for work, the school my children attend, the grocery store that is conveniently located on my way home. These things matter to God and I have, by virtue of my *feminine personhood*, the opportunity to affect these people and places for good! What might that look like?

A Helper Who Is a Hedge

My sister Leslie is a nurse. She works in a very busy doctor's office as a triage nurse, which means – among other things – that she takes phone calls from patients who are either ill or who think they might be ill. She typically assesses the situation by having a conversation with the patient, then determines whether or not the doctor needs to get involved. One of the ways that my sister serves her office well is that she *protects* the doctors from unnecessary interruption by fielding patient's questions and needs, allowing the doctors to attend to doctor stuff. She is thoughtful and strategic as she has a few minutes with one of the doctors during the day so that she protects his time and attention. Granted, this is part of Leslie's job. But her spirit, her disposition, is to be a "shield" in some ways for those very busy, very much in-demand, very weary doctors.

Having the disposition to protect those who work with us – whether professionally or in a volunteer capacity – means that we are concerned for their time, their energy, their reputation, and their spirit. We protect a supervisor from unnecessary stress by keeping him apprised of our progress. We protect a co-worker from missing a meeting by making sure she sees the notice that was distributed while she was on vacation. We protect a neighbor from unfair judgment by not only refusing to participate in gossip about her with the local running club, but setting the record straight and urging the others to refrain from disparaging remarks. We protect the integrity of our company by holding accountable those who work for us.

Thinking a little more broadly, godly womanhood expresses itself in our desire to be protectors for those who are at risk in our community. We have women in our church who spend themselves on behalf of people whom they do not know in order to rescue them from the disaster of abortion, the horror of human trafficking and the despair of homelessness. I recently invited Jo to join our Women's Leadership Team (not exactly the dream team, but close). She was enthusiastic and encouraged, and I was sure she would say "yes." However, after praying for several days about the opportunity, Jo called to let me know that while she would love to be on our team, she really felt the need to invest in our community by training to work with Crisis Pregnancy Center. I was disappointed to miss her in leadership but so encouraged by Jo's *ezer* disposition to protect those who are without power to protect themselves!

Becoming Eve, an *ezer* who bears this aspect of the image of God means that we tend our place – our office, or schoolroom, or gym, or neighborhood – and our personhood as a hedge of protection around these people whose lives intersect with ours, even casually. Even impersonally, from a distance. As we do so, we must remember that God is our *shield*. He is our *defender*. In spite of all that is changing on our horizon, God never changes. Because of this immutable *ezer*-nature of God, we are free to think less of ourselves and more for the benefit of others. He will protect us. It is His help that has saved us thus far.

We will not be able to "save" everyone around us who is struggling. To try to do so would be futile and foolish. As an ezer/hedge-protector, we exercise our faith in the work of God in the lives of others. The strugglers around us must know that we believe that *"Our soul waits for the Lord for He is our ezer and our shield."* Ultimately, that's the best news an *ezer* has to offer!

A Helper Who Is an Empathizer

"Show me a sign of your favor, that those who hate me may see and be put to shame because you, LORD, have helped me and comforted me."[202]

I introduced you to my friend Tracy in Chapter 2. When I began this work, Tracy was volunteering in the Bronx as a buddy for several children. More recently, Tracy and her ministry partner Sara have launched a non-profit organization to assist families in the Bronx to raise their children to be healthy, successful, contributing members of society.

Even as a very young woman, Sara had a passion for the people in this neighborhood. She desperately wanted to help them, but she knew that her very Caucasian skin would be a barrier to building relationships. Unable to climb into the skin of the people on Beekman Street, Sara did the next best thing – she moved onto their street. She *lived among them*. When Sara married, she and her husband remained on that street together. Why?

Sara knew that in order to have any influence with these women and their children, she needed to understand their lives. To feel their despair. To experience fear, and neglect, and hunger. Sara's life, to that point, had been marked by security, love, provision and hope. The only way for her to empathize with these new friends, to understand what she had not experienced, would be to live with them. And so she did. And then she met Tracy

202 Psalm 86:17

and together they have begun something amazing. A House on Beekman[203] is thriving.

A woman who is *becoming Eve* has the growing disposition of one who readily remembers her own journey and extends grace to those who are a few steps behind her, still finding their way. If the experience is "unknown territory" – like the poverty in the Bronx for an upper-middle-class white girl – godly womanhood works hard to understand what she has never known. This requires the asking of intentional questions and good listening skills and it applies to every relationship and circumstance. We empathize with a young mom when we ask if she is getting good rest, and listen to her response. We empathize with the receptionist in a doctor's office when we ask if she's had a busy day. We empathize with another parent on the parent's association when we listen to her fears and concerns for her failing child.

I sat with Allison in my office this week as she described the "politics" of her project management team. I did not understand a lot of the details, but the gist of her situation was pretty obvious. People on the team were not "on the team." They were, in fact, vying for position, maneuvering and manipulating and scheming to ensure their own upward mobility. The manager of the team, Allison's supervisor, had been backed into a corner, into a no-win situation. Rather than nursing bitterness and rehearsing the failure of her boss, Allison was able to "put" herself into his position and empathize with the layers of issues that had contributed to the situation. She was unable to *do* much to help, but Allison's disposition on the team was conciliatory and constructive and her influence ultimately helped the team to be productive.

Empathy in the office is uncommon, as it carries with it the

203 See the website, www.ahouseonbeekman.org for more information

risk of being seen as weak, or insecure, or "soft." Because the marketplace values ambition, power, and success, the idea that a godly woman in the workplace is one who makes an effort to empathize with her colleagues may be considered unwise.

Ultimately, though, our hope and trust is not in our position in the world, but in God alone who is our *ezer*. If it is His good plan that we become *like Him* (and it is!), then it follows that *becoming Eve* as an empathizer in the workplace is good and wise. Even if it's risky. We do not take our cues from the world. We follow the lead of our Father, our *ezer Empathizer*.

As we apply the disposition of empathy more broadly to our neighborhood, community and city the practice becomes a little more complicated. How are we able to empathize with the uncounted experiences that make up the landscape of our hometown? It is not possible or necessary to feel the weight or understand the issues and challenges of every demographic, every issue, every pressing need in the community. It is imperative, however, that we ask the Lord to give us a tender heart for those who are *not at all like us*. Some of us will have to train ourselves to gain an understanding for others. This has certainly been my experience. I'm just not naturally inclined to the needs and challenges and issues of people who aren't in my little circle.

To *train myself*, I have begun to read the paper and listen to the news. I want to become informed about the issues in our city – seeking to understand not just one side of a pressing need or challenge, but trying to gain an appreciation for different perspectives. Another important step in the training process has been to identify one need, one issue, one community of people and make the effort to really get involved. To get to know individuals impacted as well as those who are making a difference. While I am not an "expert," exposure to one area of need in our city has opened my eyes to the many hardships and challenges that exist here and has given me a deep appreciation for those who are working to make a difference – both in faith-based ministries and non-profit organizations. My *empathy* capacity is growing.

Becoming Eve, an *ezer* who bears the empathizing nature of God, means that we are women who remember where we've come from and how much we have learned. We offer grace and compassion to those who are still plodding along a few steps behind us and we work hard to understand those whose journey is not at all like ours. Our interest and concern, however, will be shallow and without effect if it is not rooted in our own deep gratitude for the empathy of God toward us in Christ Jesus. He *"made Himself nothing, being born in the likeness of man"* so that He could ultimately rescue us from our own depravity and sin. We will, therefore, bring Him great glory and joy as we image-bear His empathy to our neighbors, coworkers, teammates, and fellow citizens.

A Woman Who Is a Lifter

Caitlyn is a school teacher. She loves her work, both the children in her class and the people who are on her teaching team. One of her colleagues is a young mom with two small children. Caitlyn and Desire[204] became friends as well as coworkers, even though Caitlyn is single and several years younger than Desire. After some months of getting to know one another and a growing level of friendship, Desire confided to Caitlyn that her marriage was in trouble and ultimately Desire's husband left his family.

Desire was not a Christian; in fact, she had virtually no faith/

204 Not her real name

religious background at all. As Caitlyn faithfully prayed for Desire, she also did what she could to be her *strong support.* She often went to Desire's home in the evening to help her with dinner and getting the children to bed. She offered to stay with the children when Desire needed to run errands, go to meetings, or see a counselor. Several months later, Caitlyn had the opportunity to invite Desire to a Bible study for women who were not yet believers. Desire went to that study and Caitlyn went with her – even though the material was basic and already very familiar for her.

I'm not sure she would use the language of *camak,* the Hebrew word for "upholder," but if you asked Desire today, she would describe Caitlyn as such a woman. Caitlyn had the disposition of a helper who *lifted* her – held her up – during a particularly traumatic season of her life.

In our generation, for whom the "God-helps-those-who-help-themselves" mantra is at the core of our belief-system, trouble – or hardship, or crisis, or disaster – comes as an unwelcome surprise. Being a woman who is an *ezer-lifter* means that we are always asking the Spirit to give us the capacity to help in the midst of hardship and despair, offering for friends and neighbors *real* answers and *real* situations that are rooted in the Gospel!

That help may come in the form of speaking words of encouragement to a co-worker, neighbor, team-mate or friend. It may seem awkward and uncomfortable to use Scripture with people who are not yet Christians, but these are words of *life*! Who knows better the pain and agony of despair, of loneliness, of disappointment, of fear, of fatigue than the Savior who *became man and dwelt among us*? The words of the psalms resonate with expression of just such emotion; remember that the "lamenting" psalms are the largest category in the psalter. Yet each psalm also resounds with the *lifting* character and nature of God. How hopeful such a picture of God might be to our friends who are *without hope*! As we speak words that are from the mouth of God during these seasons we give expression to the Person of God and His work in creation, words that have potential to invigorate dead hearts and breathe life into sagging souls.

Or our help may be more tangible. My sister-in-law has a deep and personal concern for the homeless. Recently, while preparing for a family trip to Washington, D.C., Kim took her two children to the Dollar Store and gave them each a small sum of money. Their assignment was to spend their money on items that they thought would be necessary for people who are living on the street. Olivia and Sam, with all of their money spent, left the store with several bags of mostly personal hygiene products – but a few "treats" thrown in too.

Once they were home, Kim set the children up with gallon-sized Ziploc® bags and together they began assembling "care kits." There were toothbrushes and toothpaste, soap, sanitizer, Kleenex®, mittens, socks, combs and brushes, and mouthwash. As they packed their bags for D.C., the children each put eight or ten care kits in their backpacks.

Josh and Kim and the kids had a wonderful tour of our capital city. They saw the Smithsonian, the White House, several presidential memorials, the Tomb of the Unknown Soldier. But none those was the highlight of the trip for Olivia and Sam. What the children loved most, and what they will always remember, were the faces of the homeless men and women who Livi and Sam "met" as they were walking along from one tourist site to another. It was such a small thing, but Kim's disposition to *lift* those people out of despair, even for a moment, influenced her children forever.

A Ziploc® bag full of personal hygiene items won't have much impact on the plight of homeless people in D.C. But it's a start. Some women, exercising the disposition of *helper-lifter,* will need to invest more time, more energy, or resources into the issues and needs of the people in the community. Shelters, halfway houses, Habitat homes, job training, financial assistance, and other means of *rescue* offer opportunity for women to – like Jeremiah's friends – gently lift those who are suffering out of the pit with the hope of a restored life.

Ultimately, such restoration happens by the power of God in Christ as He lifts a sinner out of despair and into the joy of life everlasting. This ought to be the bent of our heart and mind as we bear His image in the places where we live. *"The Lord is the upholder of my life."* He has lifted me out of the pit of destruction and into the comfort and security of His family. Who will join me in the effort to lead others to such a rescue?

A Helper Who Is a Promoter

My friend Carrie works with refugees in our city. She tells me that at least 500 of the world's refugees settle here every year. Carrie's job (and joy) is to teach English to the community of people who find their way to her classroom. She typically teaches adults, but this summer, Carrie launched a reading program for the children of her students. Fifteen children participated and collectively they read 111 books with the help of one of Carrie's interns. At the end of the program, each child was awarded a certificate that recorded the number of books and total minutes read as well as an age-appropriate book to take home.

This is Carrie "encouraging the growth and development" of the children in her program and, by extension, their parents.

This is Carrie promoting the purposes and plans of God for the lives of these people. Which of those young people might gain citizenship in his country and go on to influence generations of our children and their children? Which might return to their own country, well-educated and thoroughly prepared to help lead that country toward a healthier, better established society? Carrie cannot see what God will do in the future, but she knows that *now* is the time to do what she can to give these dear people a vision for their lives that will honor Him and help His people.

The *helper-promoter* disposition, particularly as it is applied outside of the home and the church, is not always as straightforward and/or well-received as Carrie's story. This is the age of the *self-promoter*. The independent contractor. The self-made man. We've already considered the work of the Spirit that it will take for a godly woman to resist the urge to "look out for number one"[205] as it relates to our families and our churches. Our faith will be tested as we apply this thinking to our relationships in the arena of the world – workplace, committees, boards, sports teams – because the risk of such living can be pretty dramatic. But don't quit reading. This is where the good stuff is!

I want to take you back to the experience of my friend Jill, introduced at the beginning of this chapter. Jill interacts all day, every day, with men at the corporate level. Some of her conversations and meetings are with the men to whom she reports as her supervisors but most of her time on a typical day is spent leading, encouraging and equipping the men who report to *her*. They are specialists in a field of service that requires a great deal of physical labor and she has teams that work both day and night.

For as long as I have known Jill, three things strike me as

205 Recall the lyrics to the Travis Tritt song

significant in her journey to become Eve in her workplace.

The first is the respect that she offers these guys – each one, every time. She treats them not as "underlings", but as *men who deserve to be regarded with dignity.* I have never once heard her take advantage of her position, speak condescendingly, or with disdain. It is also notable that I have never heard Jill participate in any inappropriate humor or any remarks that might demean her own femininity. Jill's working relationship with these men is respectful and professional.

Yet she is always *genuinely interested in their lives*. She asks about their wives, their children, their vacation, their softball team… She laughs at their stories and shares some of her own. She is careful to never cross the line beyond interest that is courteous, but these guys know she is "for" them. She's also quick to commend her employees, noting what they do well and encouraging them to continue to succeed and grow. These men have great regard for Jill because they know that she cares about them beyond the eight or ten hours a day that they put in to work.

Finally, and perhaps most instructive to our thinking about our *helper-promoter* disposition, is Jill's concentrated effort to encourage and promote the *manliness* of the men who work for her. Jill always has in mind how she can strategically help these men to *be men,* to make decisions, to be strong, to lead where they ought to lead, and to honor and respect women. I've known her to stand by and let one of her employees change the tire on her truck – when she is fully capable of doing that herself (which is one of the reasons why we're friends!). I've seen her let one of her employees open the door for her. Often, Jill sets her own strength aside in favor of allowing these guys to *be men*.

Such an example might seem unusual. Jill's choice to encourage her employees to exercise their strength may appear to come at the cost of demonstrating her own, but it has been very instructive to watch Jill's career path. The men who work *for* her and those who are her supervisors have great admiration, respect and even affection for Jill. She is one of very few women in management at her company and her future there is quite secure and very promising. She is one of my heroes in this arena because I have so few examples of women in her position – and her *ezer promoter* disposition *shines*. She has not suffered because of her disposition to promote those who work for her. Instead, her work is thriving.

Jill's experience cannot be applied to every woman in every job or every circumstance. What *can* be learned is a growing desire to be driven not by selfish ambition or fear but by a deep desire to see the will of God come to pass in the lives of others. Sometimes this means having hard conversations, speaking truth, or revealing weakness. Doing so in a way that is redemptive is another mark of godly womanhood. We sacrifice our comfort, our time, our position so that others are able to accomplish the great purpose of God for their lives.

We are free to live such a life, in spite of the messages that we receive from the culture, because we *know* that God is *our promoter*. We are His workmanship. He is chipping away at the stone that will become our Christ-like appearance someday. God will accomplish His purpose for our lives and no one, man or woman, can stop His plan. Such understanding frees us from the desperate need to promote ourselves and allows us to engage fully in the *ezer*-image-bearing promotion of others.

As we look around our office, classroom or club, as we take our place on a softball team, in line to serve lunch at our child's school, or at the table in a conference room. We recognize the unique opportunity to participate in the plan of God for the lives of others. Through the help of the Spirit of God, we see people as *He* sees them and we long for ways to promote His purposes and bring *Him* glory in their lives. What are their gifts? Their challenges? Their needs? Their dreams, and strengths, and heartaches? *How can we help?*

Ultimately, we know that this process belongs to God. It was God who promoted David, and Peter, and Mary, and Zacchaeus. *"I have granted ezer to one who is mighty; I have exalted one chosen from the people."* Notice the emphasis on "I" – God. The Creator. The Author and Finisher of our Faith. The Sculptor. The outcome of each story belongs to Him and we can trust this Artist to complete the work that He has begun. What a relief.

Long Live the Queen

The faith-filled disposition of a *helper,* designed by God and made in His own image, demonstrates itself in her desire to impact the world around her for good, bringing the Gospel to bear on the lives of the people in the world as she protects, empathizes, lifts, and promotes them in whatever way seems appropriate. She takes risks. She thinks for others. She refuses to self-promote and self-protect as she trusts the Lord to do those things *for her*. Like Esther.

The story of Esther is full of *ezer*-image-bearing undertones. The adventures of her youth, her rise to royalty, her life-and-death dilemma and the only-God-could-do-this rescue of His people through Esther's influence could ignite several books or screenplays. (If you've not read it, do yourself a favor and take just a few minutes to read the entire account in Scripture – it's only ten chapters!)

For now, consider Esther's *becoming Eve* – her unparalleled example of a woman who loved her country and its people passionately and without reserve and who served as its *helper* at a most desperate time in history.

The "bare bones" of the story is that Esther went from being an average Jewish orphan girl to occupying the highest position for a woman in the land of Persia. She became queen not by her own ambition but because the king chose her from all of the beautiful young women in the country. Her early days in the court were spent doing regular queen-things and making friends. In fact, she carried herself with such grace and kindness that she soon became the most loved woman at the court.

But predictably, there was an enemy in the court. His name was Haman and he hated *all* of the Jews. He did not know that Esther was a Jew, but no matter. He hated her people and he set out to destroy them, deploying his influence with the king and wrangling an edict for their widespread annihilation. When Esther learned of this plot, she was stunned and almost paralyzed. What could she do? Even as the most favored queen, her ability to sway her husband and save her people (and ultimately, herself) was extremely doubtful – and definitely risky.

After several days of fasting and prayer,[206] God gave Esther a plan. It involved her uninvited appearance in the King's chambers (something that was *never* done), two banquets, and a divine history lesson. Before it was over, Haman was hung on his own gallows by order of the king. The Jewish nation was saved and the king was protected from committing an atrocity against God's chosen people. Long live Queen Esther!

Can you see Esther's *helper disposition* in this scene? Do you see the *ezer-helper* image of God in Esther as He uses her to

206 Scripture does not specifically tell us that Esther prayed, but commentaries agree that history and context would tell us that she prayed and led her companions to pray and fast also.

preserve her family, her people, and her king? She became a literal **Hedge of protection** for the Jewish people when she took on their cause as her own and risked her life for theirs. She did not stand far off from their plight (which she could have!) but instead **Empathized** with them as she heard of their impending destruction; she "*became deeply distressed,*" wept and agonized over the evil plot of Haman to wipe out her people. She **Lifted** the people, becoming their "strong support" as she led them to the Throne of Grace through prayer and fasting. She **Promoted** the purposes and plans of God for the lives of the people and for the king as she aligned herself with them and challenged the king to let them live.

These actions, flowing out of her own faith, are particularly notable when we think about the fact that *no one knew Esther was a Jew*. She could have gone about her own life, turning a blind eye to the plight of the people and no one would ever have known. But Esther was an *ezer-helper*, created in the image of God. We don't know much about her beyond this story, but we do know that Esther was raised by her Uncle Mordecai who loved and revered God.[207] It would seem that Mordecai's niece embraced his faith, and we can assume that she – like many men and women before her – experienced the covenant *help* of Jehovah God as she became a young woman. It was this faith that informed her life in the court. It was this confidence in God that gave her the capacity to try to make a difference in a dilemma so severe that it must have seemed an outrageous chore. And yet God worked through this young woman, an *ezer-helper* for her nation.

We could hardly find a more fitting heroine than Esther for

207 Mordecai was one of the Jews carried to Babylon by Nebuchadnezzar. He would not bow down to Haman, which demonstrates his complete allegiance to Jehovah God.

our consideration of what it means to be an *ezer-helper* in our community, our city, our world. She had high rank, but her concern was primarily for others. She does not appear to have been aggressive or hard-charging. Instead, Scripture describes her as *"winning favor in the eyes of all who saw her."* She was interested and engaged in the lives of those in her "community." She worried about them, tried to provide for them, prayed and fasted on their behalf, and ultimately risked her life for their welfare.

But let's not overlook one of the most powerful truths that we glean from Esther's story: it is not at all about Esther. It's about God. Remember Paul's point in his sermon to the Athenians from Acts 17? The God who made the world and everything in it determined the boundaries of Esther's dwelling place: in a palace in Persia at a time when it would seem that His people might perish. *He put her there for "such a time as this"*!

The place where I live, the office where I work, the school where my kids are enrolled, the gym where I sweat, these are the boundaries of my dwelling place. GOD HAS PLACED ME HERE. That's a sobering and serious responsibility, and, while maybe not as dramatic, no less so than that of the Queen's.

How would the people in my community – my neighborhood, my office, my gym, my local coffee shop – describe me? Do they know that I care about their welfare, that I am interested in what concerns them? Am I willing to empathize with them, to "climb into their skin"? How have they seen me invest myself in their success? What about the broader, global community? If the Lord were to call me home to Himself *today*, what difference would my absence make in the lives of others?

The New Road

Sheryl Sandberg has set the pace for successful women in our country. Angelina Jolie has brought the global community to our doorstep and her investment in the disenfranchised populations of the world challenges the status quo in most of our lives. Each of these women, and *many* others, have forged a new pathway for feminine influence in our generation. However, as women who are Christ-followers, we must carefully define *success* and *mercy* in terms that are biblical and consistent with God's plan for His Creation.

Is success for a godly woman measured in terms of net worth?

Is "power" a goal worth pursuing for women who want to *become Eve*?

Is it our aim to increase the number of companies and countries run by women?

How is God calling godly women to steward our influence in the world?

God has placed us – as women – in *exactly* the spot where He intends for us to make an impact for the Kingdom. There is no "cookie cutter" formula for being a *helper* in the places where we work, live and play. But there is a mandate from God the Father. It goes something like this:

Because I have been your shield and defender, you are able to protect and care for others.

Because I have shown you comfort, you are able to empathize with others.

Because I have lifted and supported you, you can be a strong support for others.

Because I have exalted you, you can promote my purpose and plan for others.

Becoming Eve

Police officers. Room moms. Advertising executives. Chief Operating Officers. Pharmaceutical sales people. Politicians. Junior League women.

The old road is rapidly aging, but the plan of God for men and women *has not changed.* Our *ezer-image-bearing* privilege may be complicated, but what an opportunity to forge a new road! How thrilling to live in these days - women created in the image of God to serve Him in many and various capacities, with different levels of influence and authority, income and responsibility. The times are changing, but we have nothing to fear. Our *Helper* has a plan, and He never changes. What might He do in the world through women who are faithful?

A Powerful Name

Eve. It's barely in the "Top 500 of most popular names for girls." Who would choose to name their daughter after the woman who (seemingly) sent the human race into a tailspin of sin and separation from God? Not much of a legacy, is it?

Yet isn't it just like our Lord to take our confidently ill-informed notions and dismantle them by His Word? After years of gracious sanctification, God has given me a fresh and hope-filled perspective of the woman fashioned from the rib of the man. To encourage me to wind down a very long story, my dad used to say "Land it!" So let's do that.

In Hebrew, Eve means "to breathe" or "to live." More generically, the name "Eve" can be translated "life." As we recall God's design for the very first woman to be an *ezer*/helper, and heaping up all of the aspects of HELP that we've considered, the name "Eve" beautifully captures God's heart for humanity. She would physically bring life into the world. But her life-giving legacy would not be limited to birthing children. It was instead God's intent that the woman would breathe life into all who belonged to her – in every way imaginable. What an inspiring legacy to give a little pink bundle of joy!

However, there is one detail to the story told in Genesis 3 that cannot be overlooked as we long for such a legacy to be ours. The name-giving ceremony for Eve is found in verse 20: "The man called his wife's name Eve because she was the mother of all living." What's instructive about the timing of that scene is that it comes after the Fall. The first 19 verses of that chapter describe the infamous scene that led to alienation from God, expulsion from the garden and the curse that continues to have impact on the lives of men thousands of generations later. Adam named his wife "Eve," the "mother of all living," after she effectively brought death into the world. How does that happen?

"I will put enmity between you and the woman, and between your offspring and her offspring; he shall bruise your head, and you shall bruise his heel..." This is the Gospel. Somehow, Adam had a vision for what would be and he named his bride with that in mind. She would not live with the dread of death. Instead, because of Christ, she would carry out the plan of God as it had been from the beginning. She would not do so perfectly, but His power would be made perfect in her weakness and there was hope.

Becoming Eve. This is the vision that I have for your life and mine. That by the power of the Holy Spirit and the grace of the Cross we might be transformed into life-givers in every sense of the word and in every relationship and circumstance that God ordains for us. Helpers. Hedge-protectors. Empathizers. Lifters. Promoters.

Christmas is only 45 days away. It has been more than 25 years since the scene that became the first page of this book. Chas never led devotions for our family. I grieved that loss for many years. What I have learned, however, is that my grief was misplaced. It was not until I saw my own sin, "grieved unto repentance," and began to become Eve that I realized what I had missed.

My husband has had an immeasurable impact on our family as he demonstrates Christ's call to serve, the Holy Spirit's varied fruit and the steadfastness of the Father's love. My becoming Eve has enlarged my understanding, and this has been a gift. Not wrapped in shiny paper in a box under the tree, but with much more promise and much greater hope.

I *am* a helper. The promise of the Savior first declared in Genesis 3 has made such a transformation possible and I am profoundly grateful. Because he is my

- Hedge Protector
- Empathizer
- Lifter
- Promoter

I am becoming like Him.

It seems the mountain may be a molehill after all. Amen?

"And we who with unveiled faces all reflect the Lord's glory, are being transformed into his likeness with ever-increasing glory, which comes from the Lord, who is the Spirit." 2 Corinthians 3:18